Bunny Boiler to Bride- A Guide to Planning Your Wedding
by
Lindsey Archibald

About the author

Hi I'm Lindsey Archibald

I'm a TV presenter, radio broadcaster and digital writer.

After living my life as Bridget Jones for a number of years, I finally turned the corner and looked at relationships differently, and within a year I met the man of my dreams and the one I married.

In this book I share my secrets to creating the perfect wedding and at a budget you can afford.

However, if you would like to be part of the Bunny Boiler to Bride relationship club then head to my website **www.bunnyboilertobride.com**

Each week in the Bunny Club you will be given FREE advice on how to maintain a great relationship as well as tips on how to boost your sex life, advice on how to keep your crazy in the box, and how you can learn to become the woman all men want, not the one they feel they have to put up with.

Join the Bunny Club today by heading to my website:

www.bunnyboilertobride.com

or

Follow Lindsey on Twitter @LindsArchibald

Table of Contents

Chapter 1: Congratulations you are getting married!

EVERY woman wants to get married! So if you are reading this book right now then congratulations as you are leaving your Bridget Jones status behind and are now well and truly on your way to walking down the aisle towards your very own Mark Darcy.

I've recently got married to the love of my life but when I started my journey towards our wedding I didn't have a clue as to where to start planning it.

It was a little scary if I am being honest and I wish I'd had a guide like this to help put my mind at ease and to point me in the right direction.

Planning your big day should be fun and throughout this guide I have laid bare my experiences which will provide you with tips on how to get it right as well as advice on how to save a whole load of money.

As the old cliché goes: 'By Failing to Prepare, You are Preparing to Fail'

Some of you might have been planning your wedding day in your head since you were a little girl and know exactly what you want, but for others you might not know where to start. Either way, this book contains some great advice and ideas on how to make the most of your wedding and on the budget you can afford.

Over the next year of your life your wedding will dominate your thoughts and your free time as you try to plan the best day of your life.

So what are you waiting for? Let's get started in creating your dream wedding that won't bankrupt the pair of you!

Chapter 2: Budget right and face a debt free married life

WHEN we started planning our big day I read horrifying statistics which had just been released claiming some couples were still paying for their wedding day SIX YEARS after they got married.

My husband and I wanted to have a lovely day but we didn't want to be thousands of pounds in debt for what is essentially just a big party.

Before you start planning your wedding it is crucial you both sit down and work out what you can realistically spend on your big day.

Forget what your best friend or your sister's wedding was like and make plans relevant to your financial situation.

As we planned our wedding we didn't want to take out any loans to pay for it, instead we worked out how much we could save each month and took it from there.

If it takes you years to save for your wedding then so be it, as it is better to have the money to pay for things than to be sat at home after your wedding and not being able to afford married life.

Thankfully this approach really worked for us and on the day of our wedding we were happy in the knowledge that our entire wedding had been paid for and we had no debts to settle after it.

So with all this in mind here is a list of things you will need to budget for:

Venue
Bridal wear and bridesmaids dresses
Cakes
Car hire
Catering
Decorations and Favours
Flowers
Groomswear hire
Hairdressing and beauty
Music- DJ or band
Photographers
Stationery
Videographer
Wedding rings

The list of what to pay for is a lot and this is why it is important to have a strict budget, otherwise things can get out of hand.

What I would do is come up with a budget then add another 20 percent on to it because there are always little things that crop up that you never budgeted for.

We took the above list and put it into an excel spreadsheet to show where our money was going and what we had left to pay for.

You need some kind of way to track your wedding finances, otherwise you will drive yourself crazy trying to remember everything.

When you decide on your wedding budget it is really important to try and stick to it.

It can be hard sometimes when you head to a wedding fayre and you see something cool you think will add to your occasion, but you really have to ask yourself if you really, really need it.

If you stick to your wedding budget then I guarantee you that the planning of your big day will go easier on your mind and on your pocket.

Chapter 3: Ten tips to choosing your dream wedding dress

GETTING the right wedding dress is essential!

If you get your look right you will forever be remembered as a princess on your big day. However, if you get it wrong then you could end up being likened to a toilet dolly.

Buying my wedding dress was the easiest part of planning my wedding. I knew exactly what I wanted- it had to be simple, elegant but it had to have some serious bling on it, and that's exactly what I got.

I believe when you try on the dress that you will walk down the aisle in you just know it's meant to be. I tried on eight different gowns and each one was very pretty, but I didn't just want a 'very pretty' dress, I wanted one that was stunning.

I took my mum shopping with me and when I walked out of the dressing room wearing it she got very emotional and said: "You look like a princess." That was the exact reaction I was looking for.

My wedding dress was the very first item I bought as our wedding planning got into gear. I think if you get your dress ASAP then the rest of the wedding planning will slot into place.

When buying a wedding dress there are 10 things you need to think about:

Set a budget:

As I mentioned before, when planning a wedding you really do have to set a budget and that includes working out how much you are willing to spend on a wedding dress. On the high street prices can range between £300-£3000. If you have loads of money and you are willing to spend £3000 then by all means go for it. I personally don't think you should spend any more than £2000 on a dress- I even think that is too much.

My gorgeous wedding dress was by the designer Mori Lee and it cost £650. It was simply beautiful and I couldn't believe it when the bridal shop owner told me the dress cost under £1000. When I set out shopping that day I knew I couldn't afford anything more than £1500, and I was over the moon when my gorgeous gown came under budget.

Research different designs:

There are so many different wedding dress designers out there that when I went online to have a look it all felt a bit overwhelming.

At one point I actually felt like crying because I was swamped with websites and designers I'd never heard of before because I'm not a fashionista.

So to save you the trouble here are a few of my favourite wedding dress designers you can Google to get an idea of the style of gown you want to wear on your big day.

Their prices range from £650- £4500:

- Mori Lee
- Victoria Jane

- Ronald Joyce
- Lou Lou
- Donna Salado
- Hayley Paige
- Pronovias
- Rosa Clara
- Nicole Spose
- Lusan Mandongus

Make several appointments

Different bridal salons specialise in different wedding dress designers so it's important to make appointments at several different shops to give you a taste of what is out there.

Go to a bridal store that is run on an appointment basis rather than you being allowed to just drop by. The reason being is that if you go to a shop that has you down as an appointment then they are more likely to take better care of your needs, and they won't rush you in order to see the next customer.

Usually appointment slots last 2 hours as it takes time to try on dresses and discuss with your wedding entourage what you all think.

Decide who will go with you:

When you are going to look at wedding dresses then it's important to take someone with you who will tell you the truth. Because let's face it, you don't want to look ridiculous on your big day so you need someone who has your best interests at heart.

That means if your sister or best friend can sometimes have a green-eyed monster consume them, then don't let them go with you.

You have to be able to trust someone's judgement, that's why I took my mum with me.

My mum says what she sees and is not backward in coming forward with her opinions. Sometimes what she says can sting a bit, so I knew she was the right person to come dress shopping with me as she always tells me the truth, whether I like it or not.

There is no way she would kiss my arse and tell me I look beautiful in every single dress I tried on, because I didn't.

Try different styles

You may have it in your head that your body shape suits a particular style of dress. You may be completely right but please just allow yourself to go with the flow and try different cuts of dress on.

The bridal salon owner or the assistant are the experts, so take their advice on board and try on different looks as you may be in for a very pleasant surprise.

I originally wanted a halter neck dress- instead I opted for a beautiful Grecian style dress.

It wasn't the style I thought would be best for me, but I went with the expert's advice and in the end it was the best style for me.

Not is all it seems

The wedding dress I wore on my big day was not the one I had picked out online. In fact, I had seen the dress I wore several times on various bridal websites but I ruled it out as it looked a bit plain in the pictures. However, when I saw it for real I was blown away by it.

When looking for a wedding dress it is really important to keep an open mind as many girls fantasise about a dress they have seen in a brochure or online but when they have come face-to-face with it they are left disappointed as it is not what it seemed in the pictures.

After speaking to a few bridal shop owners it seems this happens a lot. So when you are on the look out for a wedding dress please choose a few.

It's best to have at least a couple of ideas as to what you like, just in case one doesn't look right, or the style of dress doesn't suit your figure.

Buy a dress size that you are just now

NEVER buy yourself a wedding dress in a size that is smaller than you are at that moment in the shop. In fact, some bridal shop owners will just refuse to sell you a dress a size less than your current frame.

All brides say they will lose weight for their big day. They will have a perfect size in mind, but sometimes it doesn't work out like that. I lost weight for my wedding but it wasn't as much as I had hoped. My dress still fit me perfectly as I got it in the size I was when I handed the money over.

You can always alter a dress and make it smaller, but you are screwed if you are bigger than your dress will allow.

Tiara or veil?

For many brides a veil symbolises a wedding and that is why they choose one. In picking out a wedding veil make sure that it will suit your wedding gown and the theme of your wedding. Traditional veils are very formal and usually measure around three and a half yards long. Veils nowadays come in various lengths. There is even a shoulder length flyaway type that is preferred by many modern brides.

For me though, I wanted to look like a princess and I love anything that sparkles so I just had to have a tiara. I got mine from a bridal store and it cost me £80, but you can get them online cheaper. Or you can ask one of your friends if you can use theirs- that could be your 'something borrowed'.

There are lots of different tiaras to choose from though, please make sure you get one which suits your dress, head size and the kind of hairstyle you are thinking about.

Get a good seamstress:

Once you have bought your dream wedding dress now it is time to find yourself a good seamstress to make your gown fit your body perfectly.

More often than not, the bridal salon where you get your dress will recommend someone, if not then get on Facebook and ask your friends for suggestions.

As soon as you have your dress then call the seamstress and book in your dress fitting appointments. It all depends on how much work is required on the dress as to how many times you will have to visit your seamstress.

My dress was fairly simple so I only had to see her twice before I picked up my completed dress.

However, be warned that the alteration of your dress will cost you a few hundred pounds. My dress cost £300 to alter which I was quite shocked about as I hadn't budgeted for that cost.

Be patient!

At one point I got really disheartened when I left the seamstress as my gown was all pinned and it just didn't look right on me.

You just have to be patient as they are the experts in wedding dress fitting. However, when I went back for the final fitting appointment I was over the moon as my dress fitted me perfectly and it was just what I had imagined.

It is just the same when you go to view a house you are wanting to buy and the décor is awful- you just have to imagine how it will look once you decorate it the way you want, and what it will look like when you have your furniture in it.

You really have to trust your seamstress as it will all come together and your dress will look amazing.

Chapter 4: Are you getting married at home or abroad?

WHEN we started planning our wedding my husband wanted us to get married in the sunshine, especially as his parents live in Florida.

And he was right about getting married abroad, there are lots of benefits including:

- It is much cheaper than getting married at home
- You are guaranteed awesome weather
- You can include your honeymoon as part of your wedding
- You would get to spend a once in a lifetime holiday with your friends and family
- None of your wedding party will have ever been to your venue before

For me, getting married on a Florida beach was a great idea for a while as I pictured the white sand, the sea breeze blowing through my hair and the amazing views and weather.

But reality then set in. I knew I would be roasting hot in my wedding dress, my make up would be streaming down my face, my hair would get frizzy from either the humidity or sweat, plus I hate getting sand between my toes.

What made me saddest of all though is the fact my parents wouldn't be able to make the trip because they are getting older and they don't like travelling long distances anymore.

I knew if I woke up on my wedding day without my family I would feel like the loneliest woman in the world, despite the fact I would be marrying the love of my life.

Others things started to worry me too like:

- The number of guests attending would be limited as it is so far away
- Some of our wedding party might not be able to afford it
- I was scared the beach wedding photos would look as naff as my ex-friend's did
- We would also have to get all the relevant American paperwork together.
- It would cost a fortune to hire and transport the kilts to Florida
- And because we knew the area, I just knew we would get landed with organising our guests' flights and accommodation.

After a big chat weighing up the pros and cons we decided to save up and get married in Scotland- and it was the best decision we made as everyone we wanted to come to the wedding made it, including Robert's parents. It was just perfect!

However, that doesn't mean that getting married abroad isn't for you, far from it, as I've had lots of friends who've tied the knot in the sunshine and their big day was just amazing.

If you are thinking about it here are some things to remember:

Always visit your location

It's so important to actually go to the country where you want to get married. Don't just stick a pin in the map, Google it, then book your venue as locations can look very different in real life.

You have to visit your venue and see what it's like. Plus, you have to check out its location and see if it's easy for your guests to get there.

Also, you want your destination to be fun for your guests who will be travelling to see you get married, there should be loads for them to do when they get there.

Hire a wedding planner

When you are getting hitched abroad I would really advise that you hire a wedding planner who works in the country where you plan to get married.

Most of the big hotels abroad who cater for weddings will have an in-house wedding coordinator who will help you plan your big day. They will recommend where to get things like flowers, cakes etc.

It's good having eyes and ears abroad as they will know the area and how best to facilitate your big day. If your venue doesn't have an in-house wedding planner then look online and you will find companies that will help you plan your big day. You might think it's an added expense but I think it is one that really is worth it.

Sort out your paperwork

Every country has different kinds of paperwork your will need to get married. It's important you research what you need as you don't want to get to your destination, having splashed all that cash, and for you not to have the legal stuff taken care of.

If you have a wedding planner then they will really help with this side of things. But if you don't, then don't worry. I would get in touch with either a local British embassy in your chosen country or the local town hall at your wedding destination and they will sort your out.

They will give you guidance on what kind of documentation you need.

You will have to provide some or all of the following:

- 10 year passport with at least 6 months remaining on it
- Birth certificate for each of you
- Affidavits signed by a solicitor that you are both free to marry or
- Certificate of No Impediment which verifies your single status
- If you are divorced you will need a Decree Absolute
- If you are a widower you will need a death certificate and your previous marriage certificate

Get wedding insurance

Things can go wrong in the run up to your wedding so it is best to be insured, especially if you are getting married abroad. What if your venue closes down? What if one of your key guests gets ill and you have to postpone arrangements? What if your plane is delayed for two days and you miss the wedding? Or, unfortunately, what if you decide you don't want to get married in the first place? It is best to have a financial safety net in place as some issues can come out of the blue and you don't want to be left thousands of pounds out of pocket.

Provide your guests with lots of information

When getting married abroad it's important to keep your guests informed with all the travel and accommodation details. Also, as well as the information they need about your big day, they should also be aware of all the things they can do in the area so they can fill their downtime.

When we were planning our wedding we set up a Facebook page for all our wedding guests to look at. On it we kept everyone up-to-date with all our plans and arrangements. However, not everyone is on Facebook so many couples choose to launch a wedding website. Or you can do it the good old fashioned way and just print off your arrangements and compile a travel folder for them like you would find in a hotel. You might think that's a load of hassle but it is well worth it in the long-run.

Always take extra cash

When you get married abroad you are dealing with foreign currency and different exchange rates so you have to be careful with your money. I would recommend you budget for more than you have already- say 20 percent more. There are always hidden costs that rear their ugly heads, so it is best to be prepared.

One couple I know got to their wedding destination and had the exact money they thought they needed to pay off final balances, however, a few local vendors had charged them for a few hidden extras. In the end they had to borrow some cash from their parents to make sure all the arrangements for the wedding went ahead.

Chapter 5: How to choose your wedding venue

AFTER getting engaged I think one of the most important things to do first is to find a venue and set a date, that way you can relax in the knowledge you have found somewhere to host your wedding.

When we were at this stage we wanted somewhere we could actually get married at, as well as hosting our reception.

Our venue was a stunning hotel called Orocco Pier in the tiny Scottish town of South Queensferry, which is situated just next to the magnificent Forth Rail Bridge on the banks of the Firth of Forth.

We had always loved visiting the seaside town for lunch and ice cream, but when we viewed the hotel's wedding facilities we knew there was nowhere else we wanted to get married.

We were actually going to choose a winter wedding as we knew it would be cheaper, but the hotel offered us a discount if we would get married in June, as we were the first ones to book for that month. It was just perfect!

We wanted to save for Orocco Pier because their wedding package was so good.

Nowadays, most hotel wedding venues offer similar packages which include the following:

- Bar hire for drinks reception
- 1 glass Prosecco per person for reception after wedding ceremony
- Function room hire for wedding breakfast and evening reception
- 3 course set menu including coffee and petit fours
- 1 glass of red or white wine with the wedding breakfast
- Still and sparkling mineral water
- 1 glass Prosecco per person for the toast
- DJ for your evening entertainment
- Finger buffet throughout your evening reception
- Discounted room rates for your wedding guests

And for free you usually get:

- Wedding planners to assist you with your preparations
- An operational member of the events team to coordinate your special day
- White table cloths and linen napkins
- Fresh floral centrepieces
- Traditional round cake stand and cake knife
- Bridal suite

You venue will also help you out with any extras including:

- Your wedding ceremony for £300 (does not include registrar fees)
- Your canapés and any upgraded food and beverage packages
- And any special rates on a piper, flame gas torches and chair covers

10 Things to consider when choosing a wedding venue:

Can you afford it? There is no point in choosing somewhere to host your wedding when your budget simply can't pay for it. You really have to be realistic with your choices and expectations.

Can you get married there? You would be surprised how many people book a venue and then realise they can't actually get married there. It's really important to find out if your venue allows this. For us, getting married at our reception venue was the best option as it was all self-contained.

How many people can it hold? If you are wanting to invite 200 people to your big day and you find out that your venue can only hold 80, then you are in a bit of trouble. That's why it's important to find out quickly how many people your venue can comfortably hold.

Is it easy for your guests to travel to? When planning a wedding it's all about you and your partner, but you do have to think about your guests too. If you are getting married in some obscure location you have to think about the guests who are travelling there. We chose a venue that was 15 minutes from Edinburgh and had a train station on its doorstep, as well as major roads to get there.

Is there plenty of accommodation for your guests? Again, it's crucial to look after your guests when it comes to where they will be staying, because if there are no hotel rooms for them then many might decide not to attend. At our nuptials we booked out all 17 rooms in our hotel but there was also a Dakota hotel a mile down the road, a Premier Inn, as well as a host of B&S, so everyone was catered for and all the hotels suited the different types of budgets too.

Can you supply your own food and drink? If you are having your reception in a hotel then the majority of them will want to cater for your wedding. But, if you are having your party at a social club, bowling club or country house then you will, more often than not, be able to supply your own food, or you can get to choose the catering company you want to feed your guests. It's important to ask your venue what the catering boundaries are when you are booking it.

Do they recommend wedding vendors? If you have chosen a venue in a location that you are not familiar with then ask your venue if they can recommend vendors for things like flowers, cakes and decorations. Some hotels and venues actually have deals in place when they recommend particular services. For example, because we ordered our chair bows from a company that exhibited at the hotel's wedding fayre, we got a big discount from them.

Are there parking facilities? My mother bugged the life out of me in the run up to our wedding as our hotel had no parking facilities as it was on the main street of South Queensferry. Thankfully all our guests were either booked to stay in our hotel or in the surrounding area and had parked elsewhere, or they had booked taxis. To help our guests out we supplied them information on where they could park, as well as all the relevant taxi numbers and train times.

Can you get your wedding pictures taken there? Having a self-contained wedding is so much easier. That's because if you marry in a church then you will have to go somewhere else to get your pictures taken before you head on to the reception. Not only can this work out more expensive for car hire, it also adds time onto your day. Pictures take a minimum of two hours to get done and if you add travel into the equation then your guests could be left waiting for a long time. It's great if you can get your pictures taken at your venue. We were lucky in that we had a private beach that was situated in the shadow of the stunning Forth Rail Bridge which added something special to our pictures.

What time must the wedding finish by? You won't want your wedding day to end but unfortunately it has to. You don't want to book a venue that kicks you all out at 10pm so it's important to find out about their drinks licence. If need be you can ask if you can get a late licence for your big day. At our venue all non-residents of the hotel had to leave by 11.50pm, but for the rest of us who were staying the night, we could drink at the bar until 2am.

Types of Venues to consider

When it comes to choosing where to get married and have your reception you are only limited by your imagination these days.

Here are a few suggestions on where you can tie the knot and party afterwards:

- Church
- Registry Office
- Hotel
- Marquee
- Country Manor
- Castle
- Your friends house
- Museum
- Public Park
- A boat
- Restaurant
- Your local pub
- Your local social club
- Your local bowling green
- Golf Clubhouse
- Community Centre
- The Zoo- Edinburgh Zoo is a stunning option in Scotland

Chapter 6: Time to choose your wedding theme and colour scheme

EVERY wedding needs to have a colour scheme and for some a theme.

For our big day we had a subtle Disney theme running through the wedding.

We had a singer who sang the theme song from Frozen as I walked down the aisle, we also had all our table names as Disney duos and, to top it all off, we had giant Mickey and Minnie Mouse wedding cakes.

We wanted our wedding to be fun and less formal and stuffy like so many others we had been too.

I think it is really important to not take your wedding so seriously as your big day is supposed to be lots of fun.

Lots of couples are now embarking on themed wedding such as:

Halloween
The beach
Country and Western
Hollywood glam
Valentine's Day
Christmas
Winter wonderland

You don't have to go crazy with your themes, you can just do what we did and have a subtle hint of a theme your guests can enjoy.

When it comes to colour schemes it's important you get it right as you don't want a wedding that looks like a DIY store colour chart.

We had a summer wedding but we chose a colour scheme that was more suited to a winter wedding. We had stunning black linen with fuchsia chair bows and napkin ties. When you walked into our reception room it was absolutely stunning. I've never seen wedding decoration quite like it.

It is entirely up to you what you want for your big day. If like us and you have a summer wedding but love winter colours as they suit your personality, then so be it- don't let wedding planners tell you any different.

Here are some popular colour schemes that will bring your reception alive:

- Black and White
- Black and Blush Pink
- Black and Fuchsia
- Black, Green and White
- Blush Brown and Gold
- Navy, Eggplant and Gold
- Gold and Silver
- Gold Peach and Green
- Purple, Burgundy and Orange

- Yellow, Grey and Silver
- Sage, Ivory and Gold
- Dark Blue and Gold
- Ivory and Gold
- Ivory and Mint
- Ivory and Aqua
- Blue, Red and White
- White and Gold
- Red, Gold and White
- Pink, White and Silver

Once you have your wedding colour palette all figured out then it is easy to coordinate other essentials such as your save the date cards, invitations, menus, place cards, bridesmaids dresses, flowers, reception decorations and cake ribbons.

Chapter 7: Ten ways to save money on your wedding food and drink

GETTING the menu right for our wedding was one of the main things I was worried about. Food and drink is such a huge part of your big day and I just wanted all our guests to have the best time.

When my husband and I chose our menu we had to really think about what the majority of the crowd would be happy eating, but also a menu that fitted within our budget.

Here are ten ways that can help keep your catering costs down:

Limit your guest list

Most of your wedding day cash will be spent on food and drink for your guests and the best way of keeping your costs down is to make sure you don't invite too many people to the day part of your wedding. We had 60 people at our big day and that was a perfect number for our bank balance.

Have a simple menu

If you have money to buy your guests lobster or fillet steak then that's awesome. However, for the majority of couples it's important to produce a 'cheaper' but equally as tasty menu. That's why it's good to keep things simple. Choose food that is more cost efficient like chicken, also, don't give your guests meal options as this will put your costs up for sure. And, include a kids menu, that way you don't have to pay full price for children.

Don't bother with canapés

At our wedding the canapés were a complete waste of money- I didn't even get to try any. We included them in our wedding package as we thought it would be a great idea to give our guests something to nibble on as we got our pictures taken. They were expensive and not worth the money. Not one person at the wedding mentioned the canapés, it was as if they didn't exist. The only thing they made an impact on was our budget.

Make your own food

If you are having a reception at a venue where you can provide your own food then you can save a lot of money by making it yourself. If you join a wholesale warehouse then you can buy catering size portions of food that will be a fraction of the price that big hotels will charge you. At my wedding we decided to do our own candy buffet instead of hiring someone, and it cost us a third of the price.

If you are going to do your own food then I would suggest doing a buffet where people can help themselves to whatever they want. Afternoon tea has also become popular at weddings where cakes and sandwiches are served instead of full meals.

Avoid peak times

If you are hiring a catering firm and you want to keep costs down then try and use them out with peak times such as the weekends, as well as at particular times of year including Christmas, Easter, Mother's Day and St Valentine's Day. Getting married during the week will really slash your costs, even getting married on a Sunday can save you a few thousand pounds.

Make your wedding cake your dessert

You don't have to buy a three course meal. Instead you can serve your wedding cake as dessert. We found that at the end of the night we still had the majority of our wedding cake left as people were so full up from the three course dinner and the buffet- cake was the last thing they needed. So why not save some cash and your wedding cake going to waste by serving it as part of your dinner menu.

Drink Prosecco or Cava, not Champagne

I don't like champagne so that was good news for our budget as it's one of the most expensive drinks you can give your guests. Instead, we made sure all our friends and family had glasses of Prosecco in their hands for the main toasts of the day. Cava and Bucks Fizz are also good alternatives.

Limit your drinks package

At our wedding our drinks package included one glass of Prosecco or bottle of beer for straight after our ceremony. Our guests were given another glass of Prosecco for during the speeches, and everyone was given a further glass of red or white wine during dinner. My parents also bought a couple of rounds of drinks for our guests, while my husband and I bought a round too. Our guests were pretty tipsy and they didn't need to put their hands in their pockets much.

However, you really don't have to ply your guests full of booze for them to have a great time. The minimum you should give them to drink for free is a glass for during the toast and a drink for during dinner.

Bring your own booze

At some venues you can supply your own alcohol which can be a lot cheaper than hiring a bar for the night or spending money at your venue. However, many places will charge you 'corkage' which is basically a charge for them serving drinks to your guests.

If you are going to supply your own alcohol then it's a good idea to head to a wholesale warehouse to get your supplies as buying in bulk is much cheaper.

Also, if you are getting married 12-18 months in advance then you can take advantage of any deals that you get at the supermarket during the year. I also found that deal websites like Groupon are great for buying cheap alcohol in bulk.

Get married later in the day

You can get married any time of the day and if you want to serve your guests less food to save money then the best time to get hitched would be around 4pm. That means your dinner would be served around 7pm, so it would mean you wouldn't really have to feed your guests again as part of the evening reception. Instead, you can just give them some of your wedding cake to keep them happy. At our wedding a lot of our guests were so full up that much of the evening buffet went to waste.

Chapter 8: Have your cake and eat it

THE bride and the groom may be the stars of the big day, but the wedding cake, or in my case CAKES, definitely deserve a nod for their time honoured supporting role.

In ancient Rome, guests broke a wheat bun over the bride's head to bring good luck and fertility. Fortunately, the buns sweetened up, and in the 17th century a creative French baker stacked and frosted them! The very first tiered wedding cake was born.

Cake Bake Off

White cakes, butter cream frostings, columns and dazzling sugar flowers are wedding cake classics, but feel free to break away from tradition.

At our wedding we didn't have a traditional cake- we went for a Disney themed culinary masterpiece in the shape of Mickey and Minnie Mouse.

The two huge mice were absolutely delicious as we choose three different flavours of cake- Red Velvet, Victoria Sponge and Lemon Drizzle. We had a bit of fun with our cakes as we are Disney crazy.

Our cake company said couples are no longer going for traditional fruit cakes by choice, however, the majority of tiered cakes need to have fruit cake as the bottom tier in order to support the weight of the rest of the tiers.

So what's on top?

When you are buying a wedding cake you also have to think about what you want on top of it.

We made the mistake of getting a topper BEFORE we actually looked at cakes. As I mentioned before, my husband and I love all things Disney so we sent away for a porcelain Mickey and Minnie bride and groom cake topper. When it arrived we were shocked by the size and weight of it. However, it was absolutely stunning so we just kept it and it's now an ornament in our bedroom.

So don't make the same mistake we made and instead go looking at cakes first, and once you choose it that's when you can start thinking about what to put on top of it.

Many couples opt for flowers on top of their cake, however, there are really fun cake toppers you can buy, either at your wedding cake shop or online.

Cake Mistakes

Cakes are a stunning addition to your wedding but sometimes they can go wrong.

On the morning of our wedding the head of our Mickey Mouse cake fell off. In our pictures he looks a little lopsided haha

Here are some things you need to think about to make sure your cake makes an impact for all the right reasons:

- Do not frost with butter cream at a summer wedding unless you want sticky hands (the icing melts extremely quick).
- Do not put your cake in front of a bathroom or distracting wall ornament. It deserves centre stage. Plus it will look strange in your wedding pictures.
- Do not forget to cut it with a knife suited to the cake's composition of texture.
- Do not forget to talk with your florist about safe, edible blooms if you intend to have your cake decorated with fresh flowers.
- Do not let the photographer take distant photographs of your cake. It's an important part of your ceremony, so get up close to capture the details!

The Cost Of The Cake

The perfect wedding cake can leave you with a not-so-perfect hole in your pocket. I was absolutely astounded at the cost of wedding cakes. Some were over £1000 which is just ridiculous.

If you have the money to spend on an expensive cake then fair enough, but the majority of us don't. The two cakes my husband and I bought came to £300- which was cheaper than the cheapest wedding cake in the store. Our cakes were actually two Disney birthday cakes so the shop couldn't charge us any more money for them despite them knowing the gorgeous treats were bound for our wedding.

That was one way of reducing our costs and here are another few tips to help save some pennies:

- Have a smaller cake to cut in front of guests. You really don't need 10 tiers.
- Not everyone will eat cake! We had absolutely tonnes of the stuff left over. Subtract 10 people from your guest total when calculating the slice count.
- Use fresh flowers or fruit garnishes and your own supplies as cake decorations to avoid handicraft fees from the cake designer.
- Skip a separate dessert - your wedding cake is enough.
- Serve half slices and enhance the plates with fresh fruit or sorbet.
- Forgo the fondant. Butter cream icing is less expensive (and tastier!).
- Buy your cake from high street stores such as Marks and Spencer

Cake Details

Give your baker as much notice as possible. Order your cake at least six to eight months in advance. High street shops like M&S may require less notice though.

Your baker will need to know how many people the cake will serve, as well as flavour and decorating preferences.

You may also be asked about your wedding colours and flowers. Be sure to get a receipt and don't forget to ask about delivery information and the balance that's due.

Chapter 9: Flowers to make your wedding blooming marvellous!

FLOWERS are gorgeous at a wedding but they are not the cheapest addition to your day.

At our wedding we had the following:

- My bridal bouquet
- A bridesmaid bouquet
- Flower girl basket with a mixture of real and artificial petals- this kept the cost down
- Two bouquets of flowers as gifts for our mothers
- Buttonhole thistles for my husband, best man, two ushers and the two dads
- We also paid for handbag corsages for the two mums and my two sister-in-laws

In total it all came to £350, which is pretty good.

We didn't need to think about flowers for our ceremony or dinner tables as our venue sorted that out.

Our table centrepieces were huge glass bowls with floating white lilies in them, they were stunning and so easy to recreate if you are decorating your reception tables yourself.

I love Lilies and for my bouquet I chose Calla lilies and stunning cerise Roses.

When it came to choosing the flowers I was a bit overwhelmed. There are so many to choose from and I didn't know much about flowers, only that they are very pretty.

Here are a few suggestions for your big day bouquets:

All year round blooms

- Roses
- Calla lilies
- Carnations
- Orchids

Summer weddings

- Hydrangea
- Sweet pea
- Peony
- Delphinium

Winter weddings

- Amaryllis
- Hellebore
- Ranunculus
- Anemone

Autumn weddings

- Gladioli
- Zinnia
- Sedum
- Hypericum

Spring weddings

- Tulips
- Hyacinth
- Muscari
- Lilac

Each wedding is different. If you want flowers at every turn, and you have the money to do so, then fill your boots. I didn't want to spend more than £500 on flowers.

Here is how to keep your budget down:

- You don't have to have huge elaborate bouquets for your bridesmaids. A simple flower in their hair or wrist corsage would do.

- Make sure you don't buy flowers around Valentines Day, Christmas, Mother's Day or Easter as florists always put their prices up.

- If you are getting married in a church then they will already have floral arrangements.

- For your table centrepieces why not just use candles or have huge fish bowl vases where you can fill them with water and you can float some flower heads in them or little candles.

- And, if you really want to save money, you can also visit a flower market instead of a florist. That way you won't be charged marked-up prices.

After the wedding I wanted to dry my flowers and keep them as a memento of our big day.

Here is what to do:

- A couple of days after your wedding hang your bouquet of flowers in a cool, dry place.

- After it dries then choose a big heavy book. Then remove some blooms or petals and press them out using your fingers.

- Grab some tissue paper or a paper towel and open the book in the middle, place the folded tissue paper in the book then transfer your petals to within the folded tissue paper in the book.

- Close the book and leave for two days.

- After a couple of days open up the book and see how they look, if they need a bit longer then give them some time.

- When your flowers are completely dry you can pop them in a picture frame and hang them on your wall.

Chapter 9: How to choose your wedding transport

I GOT ready for my wedding day at my parents' house while my husband and his family stayed the night before our big day at our venue.

As a result, I wasn't that bothered about wedding cars as nobody would see them except for myself, my bridesmaid and my parents- oh, and my parents' neighbours.

However, my mother had other ideas and went on a rant when I suggested we just get a taxi to my wedding service. She wanted her neighbours to see me getting into beautiful wedding cars as all the other daughters in our street over the years left for their weddings in classic cars.

So with that in mind I was to get wedding cars but I didn't want to pay a fortune for them as I think they are such a waste of money for what you get.

To find our wedding cars we hopped on a website where vendors would contact you with their quotes and it's then up to you to choose one suited to what you need for your big day.

In the end we chose a white limousine for my mum to travel in with my bridesmaid and flower girl, while my dad and I travelled in a Mercedes Benz.

The cars were just perfect for what I wanted. They turned up 20 minutes before we were all due to leave for the ceremony and they looked amazing.

Here are some things to keep in mind when hiring your wedding transport:

Do you really need wedding transport?

I got married at the venue I was having my wedding reception at and I didn't really need wedding cars as none of my guests saw them. Are you in the same boat? Will it make a huge difference if you don't hire cars?

Can you walk to your church or venue? If so then you don't really need to waste hundreds of pounds on transport.

What kind of transport do you want?

If you decide you want wedding transport then there are lots of different options to choose from. Cars such as Rolls Royce, Mercedes, Bentley and Limousines are the most popular mode of getting to your big day. However, other cool ways to get there include horse and carriage, motorbike and side-car or even by boat.

How many people will need transport?

Work our how many people really need to get transport to your big day and realistically look at how many cars you need. In hindsight we should only have booked the limousine to take my wedding party and I from the house to the venue, as there was only five of us. I always thought the bride and the person giving her away should travel separately from the rest, but this is total bollocks these days. You can do whatever you want. If I had of chosen one car I would have halved the hire fee.

Have you got a friend with a posh car you can borrow?

If you have a friend who drives an expensive looking car then why not ask them if you can use it as part of your wedding day. You could tell them that using the car would be their gift to you from them. You can then pop some ribbons on it and get one of the male members of the wedding party to drive you to the church and venue.

Chapter 10: How to choose your wedding photographer

AT first I wasn't that bothered about hiring a photographer, that was until my mum bollocked me for being so ridiculous. She was right, you do need a photographer on your wedding day to catch cherished memories, but the cost of them was filling me with fear.

There was no way I was going to pay the unbelievable wedding photographer costs. Instead, we posted our wedding day on www.photographer4me.co.uk where you advertise what you are willing to pay for a photographer and then those in your area will email you with their quotes based on your budget. It is then up to you to choose which one you want.

The reason we went down this route was because on the website, instead of hiring photographers direct, you can save up to 40 percent in costs, there are loads of photographers to choose from, it saves time and each photographer is rated by customers.

In the end we hired an amazing photographer for four hours for £300 and he gave us every single picture he took, over 300 of them, on a secured internet link where we could download and print off the best ones.

It was great as I could share the good pictures on Facebook instantly, as well as being able to share the link of the pictures with family and friends so they could download their favourites too.

We only hired the photographer to do the official pictures of our guests arriving, during the ceremony and the official pictures after the service.

We didn't need him to stick around and charge us double for any pictures during dinner or during the evening reception, as we felt this was a pure waste of money as everyone now has amazing cameras on their mobile phones. Plus, we put disposable cameras on each dinner table for our guests to snap away, with which we bought on Amazon.

In my opinion, you only need some nice pictures from during and after the ceremony as the rest are a waste of time and money.

But each to their own, if you want your entire day documented by an official photographer then you must be willing to pay for it- we weren't.

Pictures are worth a thousand words so it is best to choose a good photographer. Once you receive your quotes from them then have a look on their websites and check out their picture galleries. If you photographer doesn't have a website or Facebook page then hit the delete button.

When you choose a photographer it's important to know what style of picture you want:

- Do you want traditional or more modern pictures?
- Do you want the pictures to be staged or do you want a reportage style, which is when you are caught in the moment?
- Do you want your pictures in colour, black and white or a mixture?

I also think when choosing a photographer it's important to either meet them in person or Skype them to see what they are like. When I chatted with our wedding photographer I instantly clicked with him because he was so much fun and he knew what he was talking about. He also got my sense of humour very quickly and he listened to what I wanted.

When hiring a photographer for your big day here are a few things to ask them:

- What styles do you do and what packages are on offer?
- Can we give you a list of shots we want?
- How long will it take to receive our wedding pictures?
- Is a wedding album included in the price?
- Do you have to pay a deposit?

On our wedding day I was dreading getting our pictures taken as I work with photographers and I know how long they can take to get the 'perfect shot'.

You don't want to be getting your pictures taken for hours when your guests are left on their own. I've known some couples who have spent more than THREE HOURS getting their pictures taken. This is just ridiculous. It's your day and you want to spend as much time as possible with your guests.

Please do not be afraid to tell the photographer what you want on your wedding day.

I told ours I didn't not want to spend more than 90 minutes getting pictures taken.

I also gave him a shot list. And I had to tell him we weren't walking a mile down the road to get a better angle of the Forth Road Bridge (where we got married) as my mum couldn't walk that far.

To help the photographer out we also appointed the chief bridesmaid and best man to help him round up the various people who were included in the pictures.

At our wedding we also didn't bother hiring a videographer which saved us a tonne of money. Let's face it, how many times will you ever watch your wedding day DVD?- my guess is not a lot. Again, people have such good video cameras on their mobile phones so why would you spend a load of cash on something you can get done for free?

However, I know not every bride is like me, it all just depends on your budget and what you want to get out of your big day.

Chapter 11: Do you want a DJ or wedding band?

WE wanted our wedding to have the best party atmosphere possible so it was a tough choice when we had to decide between a live band or a DJ.

I wanted live music while my husband wanted a DJ. A few huffs later I knew he was right because we just didn't want to spend a fortune on a band as they are so expensive. Instead we hired an awesome DJ to entertain our guests.

When trying to decide what kind of wedding entertainment you want, you have to consider a few things:

- Can you afford a band?
- Do you have room for a band at your venue or is a DJ better suited?
- Would a band play all your favourite songs in the style you like?
- Does your venue have a sound limiter? This sometimes puts bands off from performing in certain places.
- Would a DJ look a bit naff at your wedding?

If you choose a DJ then...

- You can provide him with a list of songs you definitely want played on the night.
- Tell them the songs you hate and really don't want to hear on your big day.
- Ask them if they have lights they want to put up, no glitter balls though
- If they do have equipment they need to set up then it's important to find out from your venue when the DJ can get access.
- Trust your DJ- they might suggest songs you think are crap but they really do know what music gets guests up on the dance floor.

If you choose a band then...

- Listen to their demo tape. Most bands and musicians will have a website or Facebook page where you can access their material.
- Get recommendations from friends or people on your Facebook about potential candidates for your entertainment.
- Check out wedding band showcases. Theses are great to go to as it's an event filled with various wedding bands who will be vying for your business.
- Ask if they do requests, as many of your guests will want to suggest songs they can sing
- And, find out how long a break they need between their sets.

Chapter 12: Beauty and the Bride

EVERY bride wants to look sensational on her wedding day.

Despite me being a bit unhappy I didn't lose as much weight as I had wanted, I still felt absolutely stunning on my big day.

It is one of the most important days of your life and you have to get your look right as all eyes will be on you. A wedding is not really about the groom- it's all about the bride.

If you are a glam girl who wears make up every day and gets your hair done every month then you will probably know how you want to look at your wedding. However, if you are a girl who doesn't wear make up that often and you aren't too bothered about having perfect hair, then this is the part of your planning that will probably stress you out a bit.

You will be wearing a beautiful dress so it is important your make up, hair, nails and fake tan are done right.

For my wedding I did my own hair as I do it well. I have long blonde hair and when I go on a night out I wear it in loose curls as it makes me feel super glam. So when it came to my big day I knew this was the look I wanted.

I also did my own make up as I am very good at doing it. When I worked in TV and we had to go to make up artists before we presented the evening news, I used to refuse because I knew my style and I knew how to make the most of my features with my own make up products.

So please do not be afraid to do your own hair and make-up if you are good at it. The last thing you want to do it look like someone else on your wedding day. Plus it will save a load of money too.

However, for the majority of brides I would suggest you enlist some professional beauty stylists to help you get the look you are after.

Here are some tips to help you get your look right on your big day:

Choose natural-looking make up

You don't want to look like a drag queen on your wedding day- unless you really are a drag queen that is. Natural looking make up is the best thing for a bride to wear, but it might look a little bit heavier than normal to you, that is because it will be done in a way that will look good in your wedding photographs. So don't worry if you feel it is caked on your face.

For me I had to have a foundation that really covered my face because I wanted to look at my pictures and have a flawless finish that looked like something from a magazine. However, make sure your base isn't too heavy as it will rub off on peoples' clothes when they hug and kiss you as they wish you well.

If you are employing a make up artist then please have a trial run in advance of your wedding as you want to know what you will look like on your big day, and if there are any changes to be made then that would be the time to speak up.

If you currently wear make up every day then please remember and remove it before bed. I always use face wipes to get my slap off, then I pop an anti-wrinkle night moisturiser on. When I shower in the morning I also use face wash and then I pop an anti-wrinkle day moisturiser on before I re-apply my make up.

Since hitting my 30s I realise how important my skin is. I used to just wash my face with soap and water and I would never buy moisturiser. But now I realise how crucial it is too look after my face.

Drink plenty of water

I can't stress how important it is to drink plenty of water. Every day you should be aiming to drink at least 2 litres.

Drinking water is such a natural beauty aid as it will help make your skin look better. OK, it won't get rid of wrinkles, but having hydrated skin will make your face look brighter and your skin is less likely to sag.

Water is also good if you are on a diet as it makes you feel fuller- sometimes people often mistake hunger when they are actually just thirsty.

Water is also good for keeping you regular, if you don't drink enough water you can become constipated and your tummy will swell making you look fatter than you actually are.

Try and have water with every meal you have and keep a bottle with you all day, whether that is when you are at your desk at work or when you are out in the car.

And the best part is water if FREE.

Beautiful wedding hair is a must

I've always had long blonde hair and for my wedding I knew I wanted long bouncy curls that were fit for a princess. So with that in mind I let my hair grow to just past my boobs.

When you are getting married you have to take your hair into consideration as to what style you want and what length of hair you will need for it. A week after I got married I got three inches cut off my long mane as it was just unmanageable.

You have to give yourself time to prepare your hair and if you are wanting it coloured or cut before your wedding then get it done six weeks beforehand.

It's important, just like the make up, that you have a trial run with your wedding hair as you don't want to be left disappointed on your big day.

Book an appointment with your hairdresser and remember to take with you whatever you will be wearing on your head that day, whether it is a veil or tiara, or cute hair clips.

I would also show your stylist a picture of your dress to give them a sense of the style you are going for. Your hairstyle should go well with the cut of your gown. Remember to choose a hairstyle that will be comfortable, and will not be difficult to maintain throughout the day of your wedding.

If you have short hair you might want to add highlights to enhance the richness of it. You may also have hair treatments or try products that will add shine. Flowers also look good on short hair.

If you have long hair then many stylists will probably suggest that you wear it up for an elegant look and to minimize the need for maintaining it. Personally I think the half-up half-down look is really lovely on a bride.

Your hairdresser is the expert but do not be afraid to tell them if you are not happy with your look, as you have to feel beautiful on your big day and you don't want to look bad in your wedding photographs just because you didn't want to hurt your stylist's feelings.

Get your nails done

When I get my nails done I always feel like my look is complete. Professionally done nails always make me feel glam.

For your wedding I would suggest going to a nail bar and getting them done professionally. All your guests will want to see your engagement and wedding rings on your finger, so the last thing you want is to have scabby nails. The photographer will also take pictures of your hands as you sign the marriage register and, again, to show off your rings.

On my wedding day I got a French manicure done with acrylic tips to make my nails look longer. On the tips I had some silver glitter added to make them look extra special. They were stunning and made me feel like a million dollars.

However, I had been so busy that I had forgotten to do my toenails which were completely bogging. As we were getting our pictures taken I had to take my shoes off as they were killing my feet, and the photographer took a picture of my rotten trotters. I was mortified when we got our pictures back. So make sure you look after your toenails too. You don't have to get them done professionally- just make sure your nail polish matches and they aren't all chipped like mine were.

Chapter 13: Essential wedding day accessories

WEDDING accessories are really important to complete your bridal look. Without them the wedding gown will look bare and incomplete and you don't want that.

Here are a few suggestions as to what you might need:

Wedding veils or a tiara?

As I mentioned in a previous chapter, a wedding dress wouldn't be complete unless you have a veil or a tiara. For me they are the icing on the cake and the one accessory that really makes a huge difference to your wedding look, and one you shouldn't be without.

Other headpieces such as combs, headbands and back pieces are also very popular among brides.They are usually decorated with beads, pearls, crystals or flowers. A beautiful headpiece can even replace a veil or tiara altogether and can be much cheaper to buy.

Shoes

I had an epic fail with my wedding shoes as they killed my feet from the moment I arrived at my wedding ceremony.

The shoes didn't have a skyscraper heel on them but it was still enough to make me really uncomfortable. They were tossed aside as soon as the pictures started as I couldn't bare the pain any longer.

So with that in mind it is crucial you buy a pair of shoes that not only compliments your gown, but also a pair you can walk in for more than 10 minutes.

I bought my shoes on the high street from a designer called Jenny Packham and they cost me under £100. They were part of her wedding collection, but I also made sure they looked like shoes I could wear again on a night out as I didn't want to waste loads of money on them.

Typical shoes brides wear are made of velvet, satin and silk. You can also choose shoes with embellishments like beads, sequins, pearls or crystals on them.

As well as buying shoes to suit your dress I would also advise you to buy a pair of flat shoes for later on in the day, especially for when it's time to dance the night away.

I bought a beautiful pair of silver flats with pearls and crystals on them from high street store Monsoon, and I'm still wearing them today.

Jewellery

Aside from your engagement and wedding rings you should also wear other jewellery to complete your look.

Just remember your jewellery should COMPLIMENT your dress, not become star of the show. This was hard for me as I wear loud bling bling necklaces so I had to tone it down a bit. The jewellery you wear should be noticeable and look lovely in pictures.

In the end I went on the website www.crystalbridalaccessories.co.uk and bought a stunning pearl and crystal Y shaped necklace with a daisy design that came with matching earrings. It cost £75 for the set and was worth every penny as it really completed my look.

If you don't have pierced ears then you can get some great clip on earrings these days. If you are wearing your hair down then you can get away with not wearing any, however, if you are wearing your hair up then I would suggest making earrings part of your look.

In addition to my necklace and earring set, I also wore a beautiful crystal tennis bracelet I got from Amazon.

Wedding underwear

Wedding lingerie sets can be really expensive and can be really uncomfortable. So I didn't bother.

My wedding dress was love-heart shaped so I didn't need to wear a bra as it had enough support for my breasts.

I also wore comfortable white knickers and a pair of Spanx high-waisted shorts, as it was a hot day and I didn't want to be wearing tights, as I would have ended up sweating in them.

If there is one item of underwear I would suggest for your big day it has to be Spanx. Their tights and shorts support and hold you in at all the right places and they instantly slim you. If you are going down this route I would suggest you buy them three months in advance of your big day because they sell out quick in stores and online- they are that good.

However, if you want sexy underwear for your big day then some bridal stores will be happy to help you out. I would head to the high street department stores as you will get a much cheaper deal there, and their collections of underwear are just as beautiful.

In my opinion though, I wouldn't bother with expensive sexy underwear because the majority of brides won't be getting any sex on their wedding night. I will go into this later on in the book.

A wedding is a long day and for me I chose comfort over uncomfortable sexy lingerie.

Gloves

Gloves make great accessories especially if you are wearing a strapless or sleeveless gown. The general rule is that the shorter the sleeve the longer the glove should be. Gloves simply provide an air of sophistication to any outfit.

Handbags

Of course you shouldn't be carrying a bag with you during the wedding ceremony or even during the reception. But still, it would be nice to have a small purse where all the things you will need, particularly make up for touch ups, will be contained. It doesn't have to be a big shoulder bag. Clutches will work just fine. I had a lovely silk drawstring bag that I borrowed from my sister-in-law for my big day.

Chapter 14: Top 10 ideas for wedding favours

WEDDING favours are a lovely treat for your wedding guests who have probably spent a lot of money to come to your big day.

You can make them as simple or as lavish as you want.

At our wedding we chose to give all the men a lottery ticket in little black boxes. However, we were panicking that someone might actually win the lotto at our wedding haha. How raging would you be if someone became a millionaire at your big day with a ticket you bought? We took the chance though and they went down well.

I sell costume jewellery on my website www.lindseyarchibaldjewellery.com so I gave all the women little necklaces in beautiful purple boxes. They went down an absolute storm. It was such a lovely feeling to see all the women wandering around the reception room wearing the jewellery we gave them.

There are lots of different things you can give your guests, here are ten of my favourite:

- Miniature bottles of alcohol
- Mini bottle openers
- Bottle corks
- Personalised sweets
- Keyrings
- Soap
- Lottery tickets
- Candles
- Chocolates
- Bookmarks

If you really want to save money then:

Don't bother with favours: Your guests won't think any less of you if they haven't got some free goodies to take away with them at the end of the night.

Create a candy buffet: We went to our local wholesale warehouse and bought loads of sweets for a giant pick n mix for our guests. You can have this as the favours.

Make them yourself: Many couples like to make little biscuits with people's names on them, or with some kind of design that signifies their wedding. Other people have made chocolates or truffles for their guests.

Charity donation: Instead of shelling out a fortune for wedding favours you can just donate a fraction of the cost to a charity of your choice, then you can let all your guests know you have made a donation on their behalf.

Have a raffle: I absolutely love this idea. Buy a few cool gifts then pop a raffle ticket by each guest and then draw a raffle to see who has won.

Stick to tradition: Back in the day it was a tradition to give five sugared almonds as a gift to your guests. This is still a cute favour idea, you can wrap them up in some netting with a bow tied at the top to create a lovely little present pouch.

Chapter 15: My Wedding diet

EVERY bride wants to be slim on her wedding day and I was no exception.

However, I was three stone more than my ideal wedding weight and I left it too late to slim down to my target weight. In saying that though, I lost 21lbs and I did look and feel beautiful on my big day. The seamstress actually had to take my dress in by FIVE inches which I was delighted about.

But, if I could do it all again, I would make sure I started my diet six months before I actually did as it would have made such a difference.

When I was losing weight I didn't want to go on a crash diet as you always put the weight back on when you start eating properly, plus when I stop eating right I get mega grumpy and my husband just wasn't prepared to live with me like that.

Instead I followed a diet that didn't leave me starving everyday but also gave me a 1.5lb weight loss every week.

Here is a typical weeks eating schedule for you to follow and you will get some cracking results:

MONDAY

Breakfast: A cup of hot water and lemon juice with a slice of brown toast and a scoop of baked beans on top
Mid-morning snack: Two apples
Lunch: A brown bread sandwich with wafer-thin ham and a side salad.
Mid-afternoon snack: A cuppa soup and two tangerines
Dinner: A gammon steak with 100g of oven chips and two pineapple rings
Snacks for watching TV: A packet of Quavers, a Curly Wurly and a can of low-fat juice

TUESDAY

Breakfast: A cup of hot water and lemon juice with a slice of brown toast and a boiled egg
Mid-morning snack: Four tangerines (You can split these up throughout the day)
Lunch: One slice of brown bread and a can of weight watchers soup
Mid-afternoon snack: A cuppa soup and an apple
Dinner: A baked potato with a grilled chicken breast and some salad with low fat dressing
Snacks for watching TV: A portion of sugar free jelly and a can of low-fat juice

WEDNESDAY

Breakfast: A cup of hot water and lemon juice with a bowl of 30g of cereal and 150ml of skimmed milk
Mid-morning snack: A cup of tea and two Jaffa Cakes
Lunch: A brown roll with tuna and light mayo and a side salad
Mid-afternoon snack: A cuppa soup and one banana
Dinner: Four fish fingers and two potato waffles
Snacks for watching TV: A yogurt and a can of low-fat juice

THURSDAY

Breakfast: A cup of hot water and lemon juice with one slice of brown toast with a low-fat cheese triangle
Mid-morning snack: A cup of tea and a banana
Lunch: A baked potato, low fat cheese and a side salad
Mid-afternoon snack: A cup of tea with sweetener and a pear
Dinner: Two low-fat sausages grilled with half a pack microwavable mashed potatoes
Snacks for watching TV: One meringue nest with strawberry yogurt poured over it with four strawberries cut up on it and a can of low-fat juice

FRIDAY

Breakfast: A cup of hot water and lemon juice and two Nature Valley crunch bars
Mid-morning snack: A cup of tea and a biscuit under 120 calories.

Lunch: Subway 6-inch ham and turkey sandwich

Mid-afternoon snack: Cup of tea and two apples

Dinner: 200g of white fish like cod or haddock with 100g of oven chips and a scoop of peas
Snacks for watching TV: 250 ml of white wine (That's two glasses)

SATURDAY

Breakfast: A cup of hot water and lemon juice and a slice of brown toast with two eggs scrambled
Mid-morning snack: A cup of tea and 85g of grapes
Lunch: Half a pack of Chicken Noodle soup and a slice of white bread
Mid-afternoon snack: Cup of tea
Dinner: Pizza Express 500 calorie Leggera Pizza
Snacks: 250 ml of white wine (That's two glasses)

SUNDAY

Breakfast: A cup of hot water and lemon juice and two grilled medallions of bacon, a slice of brown toast and grilled mushrooms and tomatoes
Mid-morning snack: A cup of tea
Lunch: Two-egg omelette with mushrooms and peppers
Mid-afternoon snack: Cup of tea
Dinner: Roast chicken breast with four roast potatoes and a Yorkshire pudding with a tablespoon of gravy
Snacks: Sugar-free jelly and 125ml of white wine

It's also really important to drink at least 2 litres of water a day to help you lose weight as it keeps your metabolism on the go.

If you exercise a couple of times a week then that will also help to shift the weight, but if you are like me and hate the gym then do what I did and buy an exercise DVD from Amazon. Losing weight is very hard work but the effort is well worth it if you look amazing on your wedding day.

Chapter 16: Top five best wedding readings

READINGS and poems are one of my favourite things about a wedding ceremony.

However, we really struggled when we started searching for good wedding readings as there is so much information to choose from online. We didn't know where to start and we certainly didn't have the time to read them all.

We knew we wanted something modern and non religious. We didn't want anything too soppy or cheesy, but we wanted the words to reflect our personality and relationship.

So, to save you the hassle of trawling the internet for your perfect poem, here are our top five readings for you to consider, the first one we actually used in our humanist ceremony.

This reading is actually from musician Bob Marley and it was amazing at our wedding:

"Only once in your life, I truly believe, you find someone who can completely turn your world around. You tell them things that you've never shared with another soul and they absorb everything you say and actually want to hear more.

"You share hopes for the future, dreams that will never come true, goals that were never achieved and the many disappointments life has thrown at you. When something wonderful happens, you can't wait to tell them about it, knowing they will share in your excitement.

"They are not embarrassed to cry with you when you are hurting or laugh with you when you make a fool of yourself. Never do they hurt your feelings or make you feel like you are not good enough, but rather they build you up and show you the things about yourself that make you special and even beautiful.

"There is never any pressure, jealousy or competition but only a quiet calmness when they are around. You can be yourself and not worry about what they will think of you because they love you for who you are.

The things that seem insignificant to most people such as a note, song or walk become invaluable treasures kept safe in your heart to cherish forever. Memories of your childhood come back and are so clear and vivid it's like being young again. Colours seem brighter and more brilliant. Laughter seems part of daily life where before it was infrequent or didn't exist at all.

A phone call or two during the day helps to get you through a long day's work and always brings a smile to your face. In their presence, there's no need for continuous conversation, but you find you're quite content in just having them nearby.

Things that never interested you before become fascinating because you know they are important to this person who is so special to you. You think of this person on every occasion and in everything you do. Simple things bring them to mind like a pale blue sky, gentle wind or even a storm cloud on the horizon.

You open your heart knowing that there's a chance it may be broken one day and in opening your heart, you experience a love and joy that you never dreamed possible. You find that being vulnerable is the only way to allow your heart to feel true pleasure that's so real it scares you.

You find strength in knowing you have a true friend and possibly a soul mate who will remain loyal to the end. Life seems completely different, exciting and worthwhile. Your only hope and security is in knowing that they are a part of your life."

Today Is A Day- Melanie Gibson

Today is a day you will always remember
The greatest in anyone's life
You'll start off the day just two people in love
And end it as Husband and Wife
It's a brand new beginning the start of a journey
With moments to cherish and treasure
And although there'll be times when you both disagree
These will surely be outweighed by pleasure
You'll have heard many words of advice in the past
When the secrets of marriage were spoken
But you know that the answers lie hidden inside
Where the bond of true love lies unbroken
So live happy forever as lovers and friends
It's the dawn of a new life for you
As you stand there together with love in your eyes
From the moment you whisper 'I do'
And with luck, all your hopes, and your dreams can be real
May success find it's way to your hearts
Tomorrow can bring you the greatest of joys
But today is the day it all starts

Yes, I'll marry you, my dear- Pam Ayres

Yes, I'll marry you, my dear.
And here's the reason why.
So I can push you out of bed
When the baby starts to cry.
And if we hear a knocking
And it's creepy and it's late,
I hand you the torch you see,
And you investigate.
Yes I'll marry you, my dear,
You may not apprehend it,
But when the tumble-drier goes
It's you that has to mend it.
You have to face the neighbour
Should our Labrador attack him,
And if a drunkard fondles me
It's you that has to whack him.
Yes, I'll marry you,
You're virile and you're lean,
My house is like a pigsty
You can help to keep it clean.

That sexy little dinner
Which you served by candlelight,
As I do chipolatas,
You can cook it every night!!!
It's you who has to work the drill
And put up curtain track,
And when I've got PMT it's you who gets the flak,
I do see great advantages,
But none of them for you,
And so before you see the light,
I DO, I DO, I DO!!

From Captain Corelli's Mandolin- Louis de Bernières

Love is a temporary madness,
it erupts like volcanoes and then subsides.
And when it subsides you have to make a decision.
You have to work out whether your roots have so entwined together
that it is inconceivable that you should ever part.
Because this is what love is.
Love is not breathlessness,
it is not excitement,
it is not the promulgation of eternal passion.
That is just being "in love" which any fool can do.
Love itself is what is left over when being in love has burned away,
and this is both an art and a fortunate accident.
Those that truly love, have roots that grow towards each other underground,
and when all the pretty blossom have fallen from their branches,
they find that they are one tree and not two.

From the movie The Wedding Singer by Adam Sandler

I wanna make you smile,
Whenever you're sad.
Carry you around when your arthritis is bad.
All I wanna do,
Is grow old with you.
I'll get you medicine,
When your tummy aches.
Build you a fire if the furnace breaks.
Oh it could be so nice,
Growin' old with you.
I'll miss you, kiss you,
Give you my coat when you are cold.
Need you, feed you.
Even let you hold the remote control.
So let me do the dishes in our kitchen sink.
Put you to bed when you've had too much to drink.
Oh I could be the man,
Who grows old with you.
I wanna grow old with you.

Chapter 17: How to write your wedding vows

MY husband and I decided to write our own wedding vows as we wanted our ceremony to be unique to us.

We wanted to stand up in front of our guests and read out our vows that came from the heart.

A good wedding vow is a personal commitment to your other half which is made clear and simple.

However, when it actually came to sitting down to write them it was really difficult.

When you love someone it can sometimes be hard to say how you feel without stating the obvious or being a cheese-ball.

Here are a few pointers on how to get it right:

- First of all chat with your officiant to see if writing your own vows is an option for the type of service you have chosen. They will also guide you to the parts of the ceremony you can create yourself.

- Write straight from the heart. Just jot it all down on your phone or tablet and then you can read it back later and fine tune what you have written. Think about promises you want to make to your partner and your hopes for your future together. Keep your vows to the point and don't make them too long as you don't want to bore your guests.

- We wrote our vows together. We went into separate rooms and we spent an hour thinking about what we wanted to say to each other. After the time had passed we then met back up and went over what each other had written. You don't have to read what your partner has written but we did because we wanted to make sure we hadn't written the same as each other. And please don't think it will spoil the surprise because when they are read out on your big day it's absolutely magical.

- You can then send your officiant your vows and they will look over them and then include them into the service they will write for you. Our officiant printed our vows onto card and she gave them to us just before we recited them to each other.

- We were so busy that I forgot to look over my vows before our service. I had completely forgotten what I had written. Don't let that happen to you as I was stressing out on the way to the service as I had had a few glasses of Prosecco by that point and I feared I would stumble my way through reading out my vows. Check over what you have written, you can even try and remember them.

- I would definitely have a glass of fizz before the ceremony to help with any nerves about reading out vows in front of everyone, just don't overdo it like I did haha. Take a few deep breaths, try and stay calm and remember it is your partner you are really speaking to, not the guests who have gathered to see you get married. Just focus on talking to the love of your life. Speak nice and slow and remember we can all makes mistakes. Just don't worry about it as it will come straight from the heart.

You can get lots of templates online but here are our vows to give you an idea of what you can say...

My wedding vows to my husband:

Today our amazing adventure continues and I will marry my best friend.
You are the one I live with, laugh with and will love forever.
I may frustrate you and deserve the odd monkey rub on occasion but I will do my best to listen to you, encourage, support, and care for you.
I may even let you win the odd argument ;0)
I promise to give you the very best of me and I will continue to share with you my feelings, fears, secrets and dreams.
You are the first and only person I've ever loved and the first person who ever truly loved me and I can't wait to spend the rest of my life with you.
I've finally found my Disney prince.

My husband's wedding vows to me:

Lindsey, over our years together you have been the most difficult struggle I have ever had to work at. I am constantly pushed to become a better person. I undertake a challenge head on and I can happily say that, for the rest of my life, I will truly enjoy endeavoring to be the best partner and husband I can be.

I have my team mate, my best buddy, my voice of reason and my play pal all rolled into one beautiful, beautiful person.

I can't wait to share our life adventures together. This is only the start.

Lindsey you make me happier than I could ever imagine and I am more loved than I have ever thought possible....it is a dream come true.

You are my soul mate and I am blessed and privileged to be a part of you life.

Chapter 18: Twenty songs for your wedding ceremony

WHEN it comes to wedding ceremony music some couples completely forget about this part of the planning until the big day is nearly upon them.

A couple of months before our wedding I'd heard a guy called Dominic Spencer on YouTube sing Disney's Let it Go, I was completely mesmerised by his talent and I just had to have him sing at our wedding.

I contacted him and he agreed he would sing as I walked down the aisle, he also asked me if I'd like him to sing a song as my husband and I left the ceremony, so we chose Cyndi Lauper's Time After Time.

The only other music we had in our ceremony was a specially written song from one of our friends, who stole the show with his funny performance. We also had the theme from the movie The Holiday on loop as we signed the marriage register- the song is called Maestro by Hans Zimmer.

For your wedding ceremony you need at least two pieces of music which are known as a processional song (what you walk down the aisle to) and a recessional song (what you leave your ceremony to).

We left it a bit late to choose our music which kind of stressed us out a bit, so here is a list of music you can consider for your wedding ceremony:

Processional

- Canon in D- Pachelbel
- Here Comes the Bride or Bridal March
- Spring- Vivaldi
- A Thousand Years- Christina Perri
- Kiss Me- Ed Sheeran
- Make You Feel My Love- Adele
- Hallelujah- Jeff Buckley
- Hoppipolla- Sigur Ros
- Let It Go- Frozen soundtrack
- Marry Me- Train
- Time After Time- Cyndi Lauper
- She's Always a Woman- Billy Joel
- Kissing You- Des'ree
- For the Love of a Princess- Braveheart Soundtrack
- From This Moment- Shania Twain
- Chasing Cars- Snow Patrol
- Somewhere Only We Know- Lilly Allen
- Can't Help Falling in Love- Ingrid Michaelson
- First Day of My Life- Bright Eyes
- Your Song- Elton John

Recessional

- Canon in D- Pachelbel
- For Once in My Life- Stevie Wonder
- Beautiful Day- U2
- We Go Together- From Grease soundtrack
- Don't Stop Believing- Journey
- All You Need is Love- The Beatles
- Rule the World- Take That
- Signed, Sealed, Delivered, I'm Yours- Stevie Wonder
- Arrival of the Queen of Sheba- Handel
- Now that We Found Love- Heavy D & The Boyz
- Crazy in Love- Beyonce
- Feelin' Good- Michael Buble
- You've Got the Love- Florence and the Machine
- Ain't Nothing Like the Real Thing- Marvin Gaye & Tammi Terrell
- It Had to be you- Harry Connick, Jr
- Marry You- Bruno Mars
- Signed, Sealed, Delivered (I'm Yours)- Stevie Wonder
- Hakuna Matata- From Disney's The Lion King
- Love and Marriage- Frank Sinatra
- Walking on Sunshine- Katrina & The Waves

Chapter 19: Twenty songs for your wedding reception playlist

- I Gotta Feeling- Black Eyed peas
- Summer of 69- Bryan Adams
- The Best- Tina Turner
- I Wanna Dance with Somebody- Whitney Houston
- Shake it Off- Taylor Swift
- Mr Brightside- The Killers
- Don't Stop Believin- Journey
- Uptown Funk- Mark Ronson and Bruno Mars
- Get Lucky- Daft Punk
- Happy- Pharrell Williams
- We found love- Rihanna featuring Calvin Harris
- Single Ladies- Beyonce
- Teenage Dream- Katy Perry
- Timber- Pitbull and Ke$ha
- Dancing Queen- Abba
- Blurred Lines- Robin Thicke
- Livin' On A Prayer- Bon Jovi
- Relight my fire- Take That
- I Don't Feel Like Dancin'- Scissor Sisters
- Man! I Feel Like a Woman- Shania Twain
- Girls Just Wanna Have Fun- Cyndi Lauper

Chapter 20: Twenty first dance songs for your wedding

- Home- Michael Buble **(This was our first dance song)**
- Thinking Out Loud- Ed Sheeran
- You Do Something to Me- Paul Weller
- All of Me- John Legend
- Amazed- Lonestar
- Marry You- Bruno Mars
- Truly Madly Deeply- Savage Garden
- My Heart Will Go On- Celine Dion
- I Don't Want to Miss a Thing- Aerosmith
- I'm Yours- Jason Mraz
- At Last- Etta James
- You Are The Best Thing- Ray LaMontagne
- A Sky Full of Stars- Coldplay
- From This Moment- Faith Hill
- Lay Me Down- Sam Smith
- A Thousand Years- Christina Perri
- I Will Always Love You- Whitney Houston
- Ho Hey- The Lumineers
- Love Is All Around- Wet Wet Wet
- It Had to Be you'- Frank Sinatra or Harry Connick Jr

Chapter 21: Twenty father and daughter first dance songs

- Can You Feel the Love Tonight- Elton John
- You'll Be In My Heart- Phil Collins
- My Girl-The Temptations
- Brown-Eyed Girl- Van Morrison
- Wind Beneath My Wings- Bette Midler
- To Make You Feel My Love – Adele
- You Got It– Roy Orbison
- What a Wonderful World– Louis Armstrong
- You're My Best Friend- Queen
- Just the Way You Are -Billy Joel
- There'll You'll Be– Faith Hill
- Because You love me- Celine Dion
- The Way You Look Tonight-Frank Sinatra
- Daughter- John Mayer
- Sweet Child of Mine- Sheryl Crow
- Father and Daughter- Paul Simon
- Daddy-Beyonce
- How Sweet It Is (To Be Loved By You)- James Taylor
- I'll Stand By You- The Pretenders
- You Raise Me Up- Josh Groban

Chapter 22: Twenty party songs to end your wedding reception

- Loch Lomond
- Auld Lang Syne
- We Go Together- John Travolta/ Olivia Newton John-
- (I've Had) The Time Of My Life- Bill Medley & Jennifer Warnes
- Don't Stop Believing- Journey
- Never Forget- Take That
- New York New York- Frank Sinatra
- Don't Stop Me Now- Queen
- Uptown Funk- Bruno Mars
- Happy- Pharrell Williams
- Sweet Caroline- Neil Diamond
- Celebration- Kool and the Gang
- Hey Ya!- Outkast
- Everybody Needs Somebody- Blues Brothers
- Livin' On A Prayer- Bon Jovi
- Believe- Cher
- Kiss- Prince
- She Love You- The Beatles
- You Sexy Thing- Hot Chocolate
- I'll be There For You- The Rembrandts

Chapter 23: Twenty wedding table name ideas

CHOOSING wedding table names is one of the best parts of planning your big day as it's so much fun to do as a couple.

For my husband and I it was really easy to come up with a theme as we just love Disney World in Florida so we decided on Disney Duos.

We had:

- Mickey and Minnie Mouse
- Buzz and Woody
- Bambi and Thumper
- Pumba and Timone
- Donald and Daisy
- Aerial and Sebastian
- Sully and Mikey
- Mowgli and Baloo

However, for many couples it can be a bit of a nightmare deciding what to go for as there are so many ideas to choose from.

I would suggest choosing something that reflects you both as a couple. Have a bit of fun with it and let your combined personality shine through while giving your guests something to talk about.

Check out the list below for some fun ideas to name your tables:

- Disney Duos
- Favourite Movies
- TV or Movie duos
- Romantic couples
- Countries or cities
- Honeymoon destinations
- Street Names
- Favourite TV shows
- Song names
- Your favourite bands or singers
- Actors
- Favourite books
- Colours
- Cocktails
- Favourite Nightclubs or pubs
- Favourite restaurants
- Animals
- Retro Sweets
- Favourite recipes
- Musicals
- Islands

Chapter 24: How to write wedding speeches

I THINK wedding speeches are one of the most nerve-wracking things you can do at a wedding.

Nobody likes getting up in front of a room full of people to lay bare their soul.

At our wedding we decided to get the speeches out of the way quite quickly, so we did them before our dinner was served.

My dad stood up first to deliver his short but beautiful speech, then my husband and I did a joint speech, before we handed over to my husband's best man for the speech everyone was really waiting on.

For those in your bridal party who have to write a speech here are a few tips:

- First of all they should introduce themselves. They should briefly tell the audience who they are and why they are important to the big day.

- They should then tell a funny story about the happy couple. If they don't know a funny story then it should be a sentimental one that reinforces the couple's relationship with each other.

- Then it is time to tell the reception audience why they think the bride and groom are made for each other.

- They can then thank certain people including the parents for their support, the bridal party and all those guests who made the time and effort to attend the big day.

- And finally, it is important to toast the bride and groom and wish them a long and happy future together.

To help you with your speeches here is my dad's from our wedding day as well as our joint husband and wife speech:

My dad's wedding speech

Ladies and Gentlemen, I would like on behalf of xxxx, xxxxxx and xxxxx to extend a warm welcome to all of you in celebrating Lindsey and Robert's wedding.

I know that many of you have travelled long distances to be here to celebrate this special day. We have xxxxx and xxxxx from Florida, Robert's Aunt xxxxx from Alabama as well as xxxx and xxxx from Sydney. There are some of you from as far away as Wemyss Bay, Denny, Livingstone and Banknock, such are your feelings towards Lindsey and Robert.

Today I'm the proudest Dad in the world to have accompanied Lindsey to her wedding, and I'm sure you will agree that she looks stunning. Both xxxx and I are proud of how she has grown up.......finally, and we are delighted she has found a good and decent man in Robert who she obviously loves and cares for.

In Robert I believe that Lindsey has found her perfect partner, sharing many interests as well as both having separate pursuits. Although xxxx and I have only known Robert for 3 years, we think he is everything we could have hoped for in a son-in-law. Mind you, since Robert takes his Karate black belt qualification in December, I knew we would get along well.

After being married for 47 years I'm now supposed to give some sound advice, but all I can say to Robert is beware of these 3 words: All, Just and Only.

Such as ......All you need to do is...... It ONLY costs such and such....... And .....It'll JUST take you ten minutes......

When you hear these words, a trip to the DIY shop looks on the cards.

Ladies and Gentlemen , xxxx, xxxxx, xxxxx and I wish Lindsey and Robert enjoyment today, fulfilment of their hopes and dreams for tomorrow, and love and happiness always.

It is now my pleasure in proposing a toast to the happy couple. Please be upstanding and raise your glasses to the bride and groom, Mr and Mrs Crumlish.

Our joint wedding speech

Rob: On behalf of my beautiful wife and I.

Lindsey stands up

Rob: We want to thank everybody who have made a massive effort to come to our wedding. It really does mean a lot. Especially to the people who have travelled from all over: from Argyll to Essex, from Somerset to Birmingham. And as xxx has said, my mum, dad and aunt xxxx have made the long journey from the US and xxx and xxxx have come all the way from Sydney via Stratford and Arran.

Linds: Can we thank the awesome team at Orocco Pier for making the day run so smoothly and for putting up with our strange demands.The food, drink and organisation has been fantastic.You have such a beautiful hotel and we are glad to have found such a lovely location to spend our day here with everybody we love.

Linds: We are really both thankful to our mothers for their participation in signing the register. Poor xxxx, despite her broken wrist, she managed to sign the register. Here is a little something to say thank you for your assistance today.

Linds: Many thanks to xxxx for being our Flower Girl. She manned up to the job of settling my nerves the night before our big day. Isn't she just the prettiest girl in the room. Would xxxx like to come up and receive this gift.

Rob: It brought a tear to my eye realising that I wasn't the most handsome male in the room. Wee xxxx is looking absolutely fantastic today with his baby Braveheart kilt on.

Linds: Thanks to xxxx and xxxx, our ushers, for your help today. The Stag do was a great success and by all accounts you all had a blast! You also managed to bring Robert back despite him getting half the group lost for a few hours! Would xxxxx and xxxxx like to come up and receive a gift for their help with today and over the past year. We really appreciated it.

Rob: *Thanks to xxxx and xxxx who helped plan Lindsey's hen do. She had the most amazing time with you all and we have got you a little something to say how much we appreciated your help.*

Linds: *Thanks to xxxxx for his song in our ceremony. It was em.. er fitting (and suited our humour). Would xxxx like to come up and receive a little something to say thanks.*

Rob: *Thanks to my Dad for his exceptional reading today in our ceremony. It was very fitting! Can we also say thanks for being able to get over for the wedding and bringing all those USDA approved treats in your suitcases. Here is a little gift from Lindsey and I to also say thanks.*

Linds: *Thank you to xxxx for her participation in our hand fasting symbolising our marriage. We really appreciate her knot tying skills. If only her roller skating was as good! Xxxx here is a little something in appreciation.*

Rob: *I'd like to get the final word in, as it will probably be the last time I get this opportunity. I want to say many thanks to xxxx and xxxx, and although this may sound clichéd, they instantly welcomed me as part of the family. Both xxx and xxxx have really been great with me, have been so warm and kind and I really am delighted to be an adopted Archibald.*

I also want to especially thank Lindsey. To re-iterate my vows, Lindsey has been the most amazing person to come into my life and I have changed in so many better ways because of her. Being part of her life has made me happier than I can put into words. So I would love everybody to stand and raise their glasses to my gorgeous, stunning, one in a billion, awesome wife Lindsey!

Before I hand you over to my best man, xxxxx, I would like to say a few words about him. He is forever telling porky pies, exaggerates constantly and is not really all that funny. He is also a little simple, so at least pretend to laugh at his gags. Despite all his misgivings, he really is a true friend. He has been there through the worst times, the cause of most of the hazy times and definitely a lot of the best times of my life. Thank you xxxx for always being there for me. I give you xxxx the Best Man.

Chapter 25: Ten Ways to Avoid Becoming 'Bridezilla'

ON your wedding day you will want to feel like a princess; you want everything to be perfect and you want to be the centre of attention. However, that doesn't mean you have to behave like a 'Bridezilla'.

There is nothing more ugly than watching a bride-to-be treating her bridal party like crap, all because she is loving the fact she is getting everything her own way.

I've seen the most chilled out women become absolute nightmares when planning their big day. I've seen sisters fall out, mothers disowning their daughters, and fiancées becoming fearful about the woman they are about to marry.

The next time you are at a wedding fayre do some 'Bridezilla' watching as they are easy to spot.

'Bridezillas' strut into the room. They come armed with a glass of champagne and an entourage of bridesmaids trailing behind them. 'Bridezilla' then marches up to every exhibitor looking down her nose at them while demanding how they can help make her day special, then she will instruct her poor maid-of-honour to grab the details before she moves on to another victim.

Here are a few tips to keep your crazy in the box:

Treat people the way you want to be treated

You don't want to be treated like crap so why would those around you? You will get stressed as your big day gets closer but you have to remember and treat those closest to you with the respect they deserve, don't shout at them because you feel like things are getting on top of you. Also, don't be nasty to the vendors you have hired for your big day. Just because you are paying them money for a service doesn't give you the right to be nasty to them.

Don't dedicate everything to your bridesmaids

Many brides dedicate the majority of duties to their bridesmaids and best man. However, I think this is asking for trouble and will boost your stress levels because you will feel like you are out of control. My husband and I were probably too OCD about our wedding and that stressed us out as well. Try and get a happy medium and take control of your planning, but at the same time delegate little jobs to the bridal party to allow you to take some of the load off.

Try and stay calm

It can sometimes be difficult trying to stay calm when you are planning a wedding. At times I just wanted to burst into tears and take a massive tantrum with people. However, that is not the way to go about things and you don't want to be remembered at a stroppy bride-to-be. Just try and be as organised as you can, stick to your budget and take deep breaths when you feel like you are about to lose control.

Be organised

As I mentioned, being organised it the key to not being a complete 'Bridezilla'. If you know exactly what you are doing and how much money you have spent then you will be more in control of your emotions and less likely to have an outburst of sheer rage. Write everything down and do your research- everything will turn out fine.

Your opinion is not always right

I'm incredibly opinionated and unfortunately I always think I am right. However, when you are planning a wedding it is important to keep an open mind and it's a good thing to consider other people's opinions. Don't just go into a strop and tell them they know nothing, take on board what people around you have to say- you might even be surprised as they might have some great ideas you wouldn't have thought about as you have so much on your plate.

Have date night

When planning a wedding it can be easy to forget about the important things in your life, such as your husband-to-be. Despite being swamped with wedding plans it is really important that you make time for each other and schedule a date night. Whether you go out for dinner or just snuggle up on the couch, just remember how the pair of you got to be getting married in the first place.

Stick to your budget

Everyone worries about money at some point in their lives and when planning a wedding it is hard not to as you absolutely haemorrhage it. When you stick to your budget and you know exactly where every penny is going and how many are left, you are less likely to get stressed and become a drama queen.

Expect the unexpected

Despite your best efforts little things will go wrong when you plan your wedding. You just have to remember that although there will be little setbacks, your big day will still be amazing. You just have to stay calm when you have hiccups as these things happen and there is no point in taking out your rage on your nearest and dearest.

Do something nice for your bridal party

Your bridal party will be stressing out trying to keep you happy so I think it's a good thing to treat them to something nice just to remind them how much you care and appreciate all their help. For us it was just a simple thing like buying them dinner at the Stag night and lunch at the Hen do. As I've been told throughout my life: "It is nice to be nice".

Remember it is supposed to be a happy time

It can be really stressful planning a wedding and there will be the odd time where you will want to go bat-shit crazy and unleash 'Bridezilla' hell on people. But please always remember that this is supposed to be a really happy time in your life. Take a step back and look at all the good things that are happening around you and smile in the knowledge that you are about to experience one of the happiest days of your life.

Chapter 26: Make sure there is no CHEATING on your hen night

I DIDN'T want to write this chapter of the book because I think if you cheat on your spouse-to-be on your hen night then you really are a twat who doesn't deserve to be getting married.

However, I discovered some appalling statistics which I thought I would need to talk about. A whopping third of Brits admitted to the vouchercloud survey that they've slept with someone else while out with their mates enjoying their last night of freedom before they got married.

And, an incredible 92 percent of those quizzed said they would never ever tell their other half about their infidelity.

However, two thirds of the cheaters say they are still worried that their husband or wives would eventually find out about their sordid antics through family and friends who attended their pre-nuptial celebrations.

Unsurprisingly what happens on tour stays on tour as 67 per cent of those who were unfaithful were on their stag and hen parties abroad.

Most of the cheaters said they played away from home because they were too drunk and things got out of control.

Others said they were stressed about the wedding and got a bout of cold feet. Other excuses included stag and hens saying they were pressurised into it by friends on their night out, while a small few claimed their future husband or wives gave them a 'hall pass'.

In my opinion, if you stray on your stag or hen do then you aren't mentally ready for this kind of commitment.

However, if you are about to get married and your partner is going away for their stag party then here are a few tips to help make sure they only have eyes for you:

Don't let them get bored with you

Have you and your partner settled into a pre-wedding routine? Do you come home from work every night, make the dinner and then sit in front of the telly? Well if this is you then I would suggest you shake things up a bit. Routines can be great but they can also become boring. Why not surprise your partner with an awesome meal you have cooked? Or you could dress up in your favourite lingerie and surprise them when they get home. The pair of you could attend classes together, whether that be exercise classes, dance classes or learning a language. Whatever you do just break the routine and spice things up.

You haven't had as much sex lately

Sex plays a really big part in a happy, healthy relationship and if you aren't having as much lately then it's probably time you addressed the situation. Don't get me wrong, in every long-term relationship there are sex lulls for a number of reasons including stress at work, family dramas and tiredness. However, it's important you are aware of the situation and tackle it. Arrange a 'date night' every week where the pair of you can switch off and turn each other on.

Initiate sex

If you never initiate sex with your partner then give it a go. Everyone wants to feel wanted and desired. Your partner could end up getting a bit fed up if they are the ones initiating sex all the time. When you first got together you were no doubt having sex all the time but as a relationship continues that flame of passion can dampen down, so it's up to you to keep it alive. If you have a regular sex life it goes a long way to keeping you both in a happy place. Also, shake up your sex routine by doing some of the sexy things you used to do when you first met.

Girls, don't become a control freak and nag your partner

Be the girlfriend men live for, not the one they will simply put up with. Nagging your partner is a sure fire way of putting distance between the two of you and sending him into the arms of another woman. Let him watch the football when they want, if he wants to go out with his friends then don't make a big deal of it. If they want you to go to a family event then don't moan about it. Make sure he knows just how awesome you are by giving him all the support he requires and he will only be too willing to please you.

Give them time to do their own thing

Try to keep your dependence and independence in balance. Tell your partner how much you need them, but don't get too dependent on them and cling to them all the time, as that can make your partner feel trapped. On the flip side of this, don't allow your partner to think you don't need them, by going or doing things without them. Try to keep a happy and healthy balance between the two.

Don't let him forget you exist

As I mentioned it's important not to smother your partner but it is also important to let them know that they are in a relationship with you. If they are out with friends or working late then text them and let them know you love them, but don't question your partner and ask them when they are coming home. It's always good to let them know there is a hot date waiting for them at home. Use your love to force naughty thoughts out of their minds.

Make sure they know how much you love and appreciate them

When you are planning a wedding it can take over your life and you can end up taking your partner for granted and, in turn, end up spending less time with them. It's important you remember the person you are going to tie the knot with and remind yourself why you love them. You really need to show them how much you care and need them in your life. That's because the majority of people who cheat say they felt unappreciated and unloved by their partner at the time of their infidelity.

Make them aware that cheating is a deal breaker

If you let your partner know at the beginning of your relationship that if they cheat on you then that will be the end of the pair of you, then that should be enough to keep them from straying. Just be clear with them that you won't tolerate that kind of behaviour as you are worth so much more.

The best deterrent to cheating is finding the right partner.

Chapter 27: Should you get a prenup?

MOST young couples say they wouldn't think twice about signing a prenup ahead of their wedding day.

Research from family law specialists Slater and Gordon shows prenuptial agreements are no longer just for the rich and famous.

More than half of under-35s they talked to see a prenuptial as 'completely normal' these days, with a third saying they would sign one.

The top reason to sign one was to protect their assets or those of their parents, many also didn't want to look like 'money grabbers'.

A prenuptial agreement was also seen as a way to prevent some heartache when things go wrong and 10 percent of divorcees included in the poll say they wished they had had a prenup drawn up when they were getting married.

When couples break up things can get nasty and bitter, especially when it comes to money.

If you are getting married and have a few pennies in the bank then you should consider a prenup as it offers you protection and could save you and your spouse from spending serious money in court proceedings in the future.

Here are a few tips on how to get it right:

Don't do it yourself

The Internet is full of templates that offer you a quick way of drawing up a prenup without the hassle of lawyers, but I would avoid them at all cost. If you have a lot of assets then it is no time to be tight with the cash and get a cheap prenup. They aren't cheap to get but it will save you loads of money in the event of a divorce.

You both need a lawyer

The only way to get a good prenup is to find yourself a lawyer. You will both need one as they will look after your monetary interests and make sure you both get a fair agreement. Remember and take their advice as they know what they are talking about. A prenup will cost a fair bit of money but it is worth it in the long run.

Keep things simple

A prenup isn't about who gets the TV or bed, it's about who will get the large assets in your life. Don't get bogged down by silly details.

Stick to the following:

- Who owns what property?
- Who gets what with inheritance?
- Who pays what bills and debt?
- Who gets the dog or cat?

Keep things clear and simple and it will limit the opportunity for your partner's lawyer to exploit loopholes.

Don't use your lawyer as a shoulder to cry on:

A lawyer loves a phone call from a client- because it makes them money. Don't call them because you are feeling emotional and need a shoulder to cry on, instead chat to your family and friends. Only call your solicitor if you have a legal question, otherwise it will cost you a fortune.

Fingers crossed though that the prenup you sign won't ever see the light of day, but it is better to be safe than sorry.

Chapter 28: What to do the week of your wedding

WHEN the week of your wedding arrives so will the butterflies in your tummy.

Throughout the whole planning of our wedding I was as calm as a cucumber- that was until the last seven days leading up to the event.

I began to panic because things seemed to be running too smoothly and then doubt began to set in as I wondered if we had remembered to organise everything.

So in order to calm your nerves and allow you to enjoy the week running up to your wedding there are certain things I would suggest you do:

Pick up your dress

I picked up my gown from the alterations shop at the begging of my wedding week. I always felt as long as I had my beautiful dress then I wouldn't care if other things weren't perfect. When you pick up your dress remember to hire a hoop for under it. You would be amazed how many brides totally forget about their underskirt that will make their dress sit right. However, be prepared to pay for it as mine cost £35 to hire for the day.

Speak to all your vendors

The best way to settle your last minute nerves is to quickly contact all your vendors to check in with them and to make sure all your times and requirements are in their diaries. When you book something a year in advance it is easy to forget exactly what you have ordered. Don't think you are being stupid by doing this as vendors get it all the time.

Finalise guest list and numbers with your venue and caterers

In the week running up to our wedding we discovered we had an extra guest coming after their acceptance card got lost in the post. I freaked out because venues need the exact numbers weeks in advance. However, it is important just to do a final numbers check and then give the green light to your caterers about how many people you actually have coming.

Send your itinerary to your bridal party

By now your entire day will be all planned out and you should have a document which will detail every single event taking place on your big day. It's important that all your bridesmaids, best man, ushers and parents have an idea as to what is happening so I think it is wise to email them all with a copy of your wedding itinerary. Don't worry as it won't ruin the surprise of your big day- it will only make it better as everyone will be signing from the same wedding sheet.

Delegate on-the-day tasks

When it comes to the actual wedding day don't be scared to delegate tasks to your bridal party. On the morning of our big day all the men who were wearing kilts discovered they needed cuff-links for their hired shirts. Instead of panicking, my dad went out and bought them for everyone. My bridesmaid also took my little flower girl under her wing to allow me time to get ready and relax before we had to leave for the service. It's just little things but delegating makes such a difference as it will ease the stress levels.

Make a photo list for the photographer

As a journalist I can safely say that I have never worked with a photographer who is quick. They take a million pictures in the attempt to capture the perfect image. Well it's your wedding day and you don't want to be standing around for up to three hours while you and your bridal party smile for the camera. The best thing to do is to create a list of the kind of pictures you want. Do you want a group one with all your guests? Do you want one with your entire bridal party? Do you want one with just your parents? It is up to you what kind of pictures you want so it's best telling the photographer.

Have a full dress rehearsal

A lot of couples have a full dress rehearsal of their wedding ceremony a couple of days before the big event. If you are getting married in a church then sometimes it's a good idea. Having a rehearsal takes the stress out of the situation as you are safe in the knowledge that everyone involved knows exactly what they should be doing and where they should be standing. I didn't have a rehearsal but everything turned out brilliant as our hotel had an amazing wedding coordinator. So don't worry if you don't have time to fit one in.

Pack for your honeymoon or overnight stay

As well as your wedding to think about there is also the honeymoon, if you are lucky enough to be going on one. We decided to go on a mini-moon for a week to Tenerife as my uncle has an apartment there. I just threw some summer dresses in the suitcase and I was good to go. However, if you take ages to pack for holiday then I would suggest you do this at the start of your wedding week. We also had to pack the kilts, candy buffet, favours and wedding cakes to take to our venue. The cars were packed to the gunnels with all our wedding goodies.

Get your honeymoon currency and print boarding passes

When you are in the midst of your wedding circus it can be easy to forget about the small things. I totally forgot about getting currency for our mini-moon, instead I had to get our Euros at the airport. Thankfully though, my husband was in charge of printing off our board passes. Again, I would make sure this is all done at the beginning of your wedding week. That way you can pack your boarding passes and currency in your carry on luggage and you will be all ready to go.

Book a pamper session

It's important for the bride to look her best on her big day and if you are too stressed it can show on your face. The day before your wedding I would suggest you relax and book some treatments for yourself to calm your nerves. Grab a massage, get your fake tan done, go get your nails done or even book an afternoon tea for you and your mum or bridesmaids and have a nice few hours before your big day arrives.

Chapter 29: How to stay calm on your wedding day

WHEN your wedding day finally arrives you will be bursting with excitement.

The best day of your life is finally here and you will want to savour every minute of it. That's why the last thing you want to be is stressed.

Here are my top ten tips to staying calm on your big day:

Try and get plenty of sleep

On the eve of your wedding it is important to get as much sleep as you can because your wedding day will be really awesome but also really tiring. Also, you don't want to wake up in the morning looking shattered with huge bags under your eyes. The night before my wedding I spent it with my 10-year-old niece and we watched Disney's Frozen, ate pizza and were in bed for 10.30pm.

Have breakfast and lunch before your ceremony

When your big day arrives so much will be running through your head but please don't forget to eat.

I got up with my flower girl and we had rolls and sausage then at lunchtime my mother made an amazing buffet which was enough to feed the entire street.

I wasn't particularly hungry, especially as I was worried about fitting into my tight dress, but I still ate something as I knew it would be 6pm when we next got any food, and when I'm hungry I'm grumpy and I didn't want that on my big day.

Also, food lines your stomach and if you are planning to drink a few bubbles before dinner then it's best you get prepared.

Delegate, Delegate, Delegate

You have bridesmaids for a reason- so you can delegate duties to them. I was absolutely delighted when my chief bridesmaid showed up because she took my little flower girl under her wing and did her hair and make-up leaving me to get on with getting ready. It was the help I needed as I felt things were getting on top of me as I had to help my brother put his kilt on as well as deal with my mum's neighbours dropping by while looking after a 10-year-old. It's really important that you delegate some duties to other people in your bridal party as it lightens the load.

Enjoy a glass of Bucks Fizz as you get ready

As you and your bridesmaids get ready why not treat yourselves to a glass of Bucks Fizz? I wish my mother had got the memo, as she was plying us with Prosecco, I think she thought it was a repeat of my hen weekend. I had a couple of LARGE glasses of Prosecco and I was beginning to feel a bit tipsy so I had to slow down a bit. Don't get drunk before you even reach your ceremony as I was struggling to read my vows haha.

If you are feeling nervous then talk about it

Don't bottle up your feelings on your wedding day. It's a really emotional time and if you hide your nerves or how you are feeling then the tension and stress will really build up until you probably snap at someone. I was getting a bit stressed and I blew my top at my brother when he came into my room when I was putting my make up on to ask me to do up his kilt shoes. I lost the plot and told him to fuck off. If I had of let people know how I was feeling, then I would have felt and behaved much better.

Speak to your husband-to-be on the phone in the morning

I think it is important to speak to your husband-to-be on the morning of your wedding as it will calm you down. At the end of the day, the pair of you are in the middle of this crazy wedding circus and it's good just to touch base and chat to your man. My husband and I were apart for over a day and I was really missing him by that point, so to speak to him a few hours before our ceremony was just the best feeling.

Grab some alone time

Everyone wants a piece of you at your wedding and it can be a bit overwhelming. You can't even go to the toilet without someone wanting to chat to you. Everyone is different but I felt like I needed a little bit of space to allow me to take everything in. I eventually managed to grab some alone time in my honeymoon suite at 11pm. The peace and quiet didn't last long though as my husband chapped the door ten minutes later to tell me that my mum had told him to come and get me. Ahhhhhhhh! My alone time may only have lasted a few minutes but it was well worth it.

Things do go wrong- Just don't worry

Little things will go wrong at your wedding but you can't let them worry you as you will still have a perfect day.

As I've mentioned, the head fell off my Mickey Mouse cake and my husband had to prop it up. Poor Mickey looked a bit lopsided but it didn't dampen the mood, in fact, he was so funny looking it made the cake cutting a laugh.

We also had the cuff-link chaos I told you about in the previous chapter.

There is just no point in worrying about small things as what will be, will be. Just concentrate on the fact that you will be walking down the aisle to marry the love of your life and everything else should pale into insignificance.

You can't make everyone happy

Even at a wedding, which is an awesome celebration, at least one of your guests will be a pain in the arse. If this happens on your big day then just bloody well ignore them. The majority of your friends and family will be having an absolute ball, so don't let anyone else get you down. If people can't be happy at a wedding and enjoy themselves then God help them.

Husband and wife time

As I mentioned earlier, it's really important that you get some alone time, but it is also as equally important to get some husband and wife time. I really enjoyed when the speeches were over and the dinner was being served as we got a chance to chat to each other properly without anyone interrupting us. We could just sit back, drink our wine and observe everyone enjoying themselves. It was one of my favourite parts of the day.

Chapter 30: Sex on your wedding night

SEX on your wedding night is like the Loch Ness Monster- a complete myth.

The majority of brides I know will agree that the chances of consummating the marriage that night are pretty slim for a number of reasons:

- A wedding is such a long, emotional and draining occasion and more often than not your new husband and yourself are way to tired to do the mattress mambo.

- Being drunk also doesn't help if you want to get jiggy with it. Many grooms are so pissed that they struggle to get it up. And many brides have had too much Prosecco that they have forgotten their names.

- Also, you have just planned the biggest party of your lives where all your friends and family are in the same room, so rushing to your bedroom isn't the priority. Having fun with those you love and laugh with is.

- After the ceremony when you are at your venue then usually the new Mr and Mrs are given 20 minutes to chill out together before the madness of the reception starts. Sometimes this can be a great opportunity for a quickie.

On our wedding night my husband and I were absolutely exhausted and we collapsed onto our beautiful big bed laughing and chatting about our amazing day before we fell asleep in each other's arms.

If you don't have sex during the day of your wedding or when you go to bed that night there is always the next morning when you are snuggled up in the honeymoon suite with your new husband.

However, at my wedding, we woke up ten minutes before we were due to check out. We jumped out of bed in a panic and piled my dress and his kilt into a suitcase, then dragged our hungover asses to breakfast.

We did make up for it though when we got back to our flat :0)

So don't worry if there is no sexy time on your wedding night as there is the rest of your married life to make up for it.

Chapter 31: How to beat post wedding blues

FOR months, even years, you've been planning your big day. Your to-do list will have been never ending with daily decisions to be made about dresses, venues, cakes, guests and honeymoons. Planning your wedding can consume your every waking moment- your big day will never be far from your thoughts. It will have become your hobby.

So when it's over and done with and the confetti settles you will be left with a big hole in your life. It can even feel like a sense of loss and the come down can leave you feeling low.

Wedding withdrawal can strike without warning- you can get it immediately after your service, the morning after your nuptials or gradually in the weeks that follow walking down the aisle.

But remember you have just married the love of your life, it's the beginning of a new chapter together and there is no need to feel sad or depressed. You have to stop thinking your wedding is the best it's ever going to get and view it instead as an exciting beginning.

Thankfully there are a number of things you can do to help put your wedding planning days behind you:

Discover a new hobby

Get out there and find a new pastime to immerse yourself in. Take up running or exercise classes, go salsa dancing, take up cookery classes, learn a new language. Whatever you do it's important to dive into your new hobby and keep your mind occupied. The best thing to do is actually start an activity before your wedding even arrives as it will make the transition even easier when your wedding is over.

Do things with your new husband

Yes that's right you have a husband now and it's important you spend time with him and make him feel loved as he will no doubt have felt a bit neglected while you were behaving like 'Bridezilla'. It's time to get on with your life together and do awesome things to have fun. Why don't you both train for a 10k, bake together, go on long walks or plan for your next holiday?

Talk to other recently married women:

If you surf the Internet you will see you are not alone at feeling down once your wedding is over. Women all over the world and from all walks of life are chatting online about the post wedding come down. Why not share your experience with them as your mum and best friend might not understand how you feel fully. Who knows, you could even meet some new friends from a meeting of minds.

Put to bed any unfinished post wedding tasks

When you get back from your honeymoon there will no doubt be a few wedding loose ends to tie up. You will have wedding pictures to choose for your album, thank you cards to write and gift vouchers to spend. Try and get as much of those things done as soon as possible to allow you to get on with your day-to-day life.

Chill out

Give yourself a break and allow yourself to relax. It's been a whirlwind of a year. You've had a to-do list as long as your arm to get through, countless decisions to make and endless payments to settle, so now it's time to give your body and mind a break. You will have gone through a roller coaster of emotions- you will have been excited, nervous, tired, and stressed and all those feelings at once can take its toll on a person.

Keep the romance going

Remember just because you are married it doesn't mean you stop trying on the romance front. A lot of women, and some men, think that just because they have a ring on their finger then they don't have to work at their relationship. That kind of attitude will lead you straight to the divorce courts so it's important to keep the romance alive. Remind yourself why you married your husband and take some time to appreciate him. Make sure you have a 'date night' at least once a week where you both turn off your mobile phones and do something together- that could be dinner at home or a night on the town. Whatever it is it needs to be something that allows you to reconnect and talk about something other than wedding plans.

Plan for other awesome events in your life

When the honeymoon is over and it's back to the drudge of everyday life then reality can hit you like a tonne of bricks so it's important to look forward to something. If your birthday is coming up then plan to do something. Throw a dinner party or book a new holiday. If you both want to start a family then make exciting plans to do that. If you need to decorate your new marital home then pick up a paintbrush. Just get rid of the wedding magazines and look forward to something new.

Take off the rose tinted specks

When looking back on planning your wedding you can remember it as an exciting experience that was filled with laughs along the way. But wait a minute, was it really like that? Planning a wedding can be one of the most stressful things in your life. You have to diet, make difficult choices, watch your budget, please everyone and listen to your husband-to-be going on about the expense of it all. It's time to take those rose tinted specks off and realise that putting wedding planning behind you is a good thing. Make a list of the things you can now do that you couldn't do while planning your big day and go and do them.

Relive your big day

Some women just can't let go of their wedding day straight away. The excitement was just too good to forget. If this is you then why not have a night with your pals and go through your wedding photos and watch the DVD of the big day. However, once you've done this then it really is time to move on and get your life back.

Wedding withdrawal can happen to anyone as the bubble you have been living in has finally popped and you have been hit by a big dose of reality.

But don't worry as the post wedding woes will eventually disappear and within a few weeks you will be back to your old self again.

Chapter 32: Ten things to do after your wedding

WHEN your wedding is over your will be bombarded with mixed emotions and one of them will be absolute relief.

When my husband and I woke up the next morning in our honeymoon suite we both felt like a weight had been lifted from our shoulders. It was a sense of being free. We no longer had to worry about things to pay for or things to pick up for our big day.

There was also a feeling of excitement, but before married life can properly kick in there are certain things you will have to tick off your to do list once and for all.

Here are my top ten loose ends to tie up:

Enjoy post wedding breakfast with your husband

The post wedding breakfast was one of the best things about our wedding weekend. We didn't ask people to be there at the same time as us but when we went for our fry up my parents were in the restaurant, my brother and his fiancé and three of our best friends and their partners were there too. What a laugh we had reminiscing about the awesome wedding night before. It was so relaxed and so much fun that I didn't want to leave our hotel that day.

Get home and sift through your gifts and cards

Once we left our hotel we headed straight back home to our flat. When I got there my husband had decorated the place with balloons and flowers. It was absolutely perfect. We then got showered and jumped into our pyjamas, opened a bottle of Prosecco and we spent a brilliant few hours opening our presents, reading our cards and going through the lovely messages left by our guests in our wedding album. It was such a lovely afternoon.

Write your thank you cards

Once you have gone through all your gifts and cards then you will have to turn your attention to writing your thank you cards. To save a load of hassle we got cards that were already printed and so all we had to do was pop people's names on them.
Thank you cards are really important because they make your guests feel appreciated, especially when they have probably bought you an expensive gift and spent a load of money to actually be at your big day.

Take care of legalities

We were lucky as the marriage registration office where we needed to submit all our documents was a couple of doors down from our venue, so the day after the wedding we posted them through the door before we left. They then processed all the documents and then posted our marriage certificate to us. This is one thing you can't forget to do after you get married. Make sure you do it ASAP and then you won't forget about it then discover months down the line you haven't got a marriage certificate.

Return all your hired items and clothes

If you have hired things for your wedding then you will want to get them back to their rightful owners as soon as you can. We gathered up everyone's kilts and two days after the wedding we bundled them into the car and took them back to the hire shop.
We only did it ourselves because we lived near the shop, but this is probably a task you can give to your best man or bridesmaid to complete.

Dry-clean your wedding dress

It's such a shame we get to wear our stunning dress only once. I was gutted when I had to take mine off as I felt like an absolute princess in it.

After a week I sent my dress to get dry-cleaned as during my wedding day the bottom of it got a bit grubby as I wandered about, my brother was steaming drunk and managed to spill some booze down the side of it too.

What to do with your wedding dress it up to you, mines is now hanging in my wardrobe until we move house and I intend to get it framed and hang it in my dressing room.

Many brides are also now embarking on the American craze of 'Trashing the Dress', where you get dressed up as a bride once more and then a photographer takes pictures of you doing something crazy in your dress like swimming in a river or playing paint-ball. My mother would kill me if I decided to do something like that.

Sort our your wedding pictures

Our photographer was quick off the mark and we had an internet link to all 362 of our wedding pictures less than a week later. My husband and I sifted through them, put loads on Facebook and then chose the ones we wanted to put in a picture album.

We also posted the link to all our pictures on our closed wedding Facebook page for all our guests to see for themselves and they could download the ones they wanted too.

Close down your wedding Facebook page

This was a really sad thing to do- closing down our wedding Facebook page. It had been so much fun in the run up to our big day as we posted weekly updates on our page to allow guests to join in on our pre-wedding journey. A lot of couples also set up their own wedding websites, but when it's all over it is time to hit delete and move on to another awesome project.

Social media your vendors

If you received good service from your wedding vendors then I think it's good to give something back in the shape of a positive review.

When all the fuss surrounding the wedding died down and I finally caught my breath, I decided to give a few of my vendors testimonials such as our amazing hotel, singer, DJ and chair cover company. I also passed on details of where I bought certain things to other couples who were getting hitched. It's nice to be nice.

Go on honeymoon

We didn't head off on honeymoon straight away after our wedding. We waited a week so that we could spend as much time as we could with the friends and family who had travelled from abroad to see us getting married. Going on honeymoon is one of the best things to do after a wedding as you finally get the chance to relax. However, we regret spending so much money on the wedding that we didn't have a huge honeymoon the year of our wedding. If you are heading in the same direction then make sure you at least get a weekend away together so that you can celebrate becoming husband and wife.

Chapter 33: Ten ways to keep your marriage sexy

LET'S get one thing straight girls- sex and blow jobs are not just for your husband's Christmas or birthday.

A happy marriage needs sexy time. Every couple is different, but I personally think you should be getting frisky at least once a week.

Now, I know life gets in the way and the last thing you want to be doing is starring in your very own Fifty Shades of Grey movie every night of the week, but it is important to maintain a proper level of intimacy with each other.

Many think when you have just gotten married then you should be shagging like rabbits. If you are, then lucky you. However, if you have been with your partner for years before you got hitched then the reality could be a bit different.

So, how is life between the sheets for you? Is your love life needing a make-over?

Here are some simple ways to improve things without even trying too hard:

Date your husband

Dating each other is hugely important to keeping the spark alive between the pair of you. Many married men and women get to the point where they can't be bothered investing time and effort into the relationship. They get too comfortable and they get complacent with each other. Don't fall into this trap as your relationship will be on a rocky road and it will get to a point when it will feel more like a friendship. Instead, ask your partner out on a date like you used to do when you first got together.

Now, many wives might think that their husbands should do the asking, but you sometimes have to take the bull by the horns and ask for yourself. Why not choose a romantic activity like a candlelit dinner in a sexy restaurant, a night in a hotel or a movie or comedy night.

Carry Out Some Romantic Gestures

When it comes to being romantic many women make the mistake of thinking it is up to the men. Wrong- it takes two people in a relationship to make it work. One of the easiest ways of getting that loving feeling back is showing some romantic gestures. When out shopping with your husband why not hold his hand? When you walk by them in the house then grab them and give them a kiss. Make sure you tell your partner you love them last thing before you fall asleep at night or pop a note in his bag telling him you can't wait to see him when he gets home from work.

Be Sexy and Seductive

When was the last time you went out and bought some lingerie to turn your man on and make you feel sexy? If you have been in the relationship for a while you probably won't remember. Well make it your mission to buy some sexy nightwear to get the romance going between you again. Also, don't always wait for your husband to initiate sex, get frisky and watch his amazed but excited reaction. Why not perform a striptease for your partner or just start massaging their body. You may be surprised just how easy and effective it is to be sexy and seductive.

Be Spontaneous

If you have a routine when it comes to sex then switch things up a bit. Change your sex positions, experiment with new ones. Why not surprise your partner when he comes home from work by just wearing your lingerie when he walks through the door. Also, don't always have sex in the bedroom, try every room in your house. Send some saucy texts or leave him post-it notes telling him what you plan on doing to him when you see him next. Why not introduce some toys into the bedroom to spice things up? Remember that experimenting in the bedroom doesn't have to mean you feeling uncomfortable, just do what you feel is appropriate in your relationship.

It's easy for any relationship to go stale at some point and it really does take time and effort to keep the relationship fun and sexy.

Chapter 34: Your wedding timeline explained

What you need to do 12-18 months before your wedding:

- Work out a budget
- Choose your wedding party
- Choose your date and venue
- Book your reception venue
- What kind of ceremony do you want?
- Book your Minister, Priest or Celebrant
- Start your guest list
- Book caterers and discuss menus
- Create a wedding folder
- Google florists, photographers, car hire, cakes ect
- Do you need a wedding planner?
- Throw an engagement party?

What your need to do 8 months before your wedding:

- Time to buy a wedding dress
- Book your seamstress
- Choose clothes for male wedding party
- Set up a Facebook page for all your wedding guests
- Get a photographer / videographer
- Get a florist
- Put down wedding cake deposit
- What kind of entertainment do you want?
- Meet your caterers
- Block book hotel rooms for guests who are travelling to your ceremony
- Plan your honeymoon
- Select wedding stationery

What you need to do 6 months before your wedding:

- Send out save-the-date cards
- Buy or make your invitations
- Order your wedding rings
- Start creating your wedding day itinerary
- Meet with your officiant
- Book your cars
- Shop for bridesmaid dresses
- Set up a wedding gift list

What your need to do 4 months before your wedding:

- Send out your wedding invitations
- Discuss music with your band or DJ
- Start dress fittings
- Ask your bridesmaids to start planning your hen party

What to do 3 months before your wedding:

- Food tasting
- Book appointments for hair, make-up, nails and eyelashes
- Finalise your ceremony and reception itinerary with your venue
- Send first draft of your wedding schedule to vendors
- Finalise your readings
- Start thinking about your vows if you are writing your own

What to do 2 months before your wedding:

- Meet or call your photographer
- Second last meeting with your venue
- Buy gifts for your wedding party
- Another dress fitting
- Check in on your guest list and do table plan
- Think about music
- Buy thank you cards
- Send wedding announcements to newspapers

What to do 1 month before your wedding

- Hen and Stag party time
- Get your marriage license
- Run through last minute details with vendors
- Last dress fitting
- Finalise your guest list with caterers
- Finalise vendor payments
- Confirm appointments
- Get your hair cut and coloured
- Have a full dress rehearsal
- Confirm honeymoon itinerary and get currency

Chapter 35: Our wedding ceremony in full

I'VE included our entire ceremony in this book because, although I had been to a load of weddings throughout my life, I still had trouble remembering how a wedding ceremony should flow.

We were allowed to write our entire ceremony and our Celebrant added all the legal bits. If you are going to be doing the same, then have a read of ours and you can follow how we did it.

THE MARRIAGE OF LINDSEY ARCHIBALD AND ROBERT CRUMLISH

Conducted by XXXXXX, Authorised Celebrant
Humanist Society Scotland
OROCCO PIER, SOUTH QUEENSFERRY
Saturday, 27th June 2015
Music for Guests Arriving – Provided by Orocco Pier

I'd like to make a couple of announcements before we start. First of all, if you have your mobile phone with you, we would be grateful if you could switch it off! Thanks!! Also, Robert and Lindsey are more than happy for you all to take photographs throughout the ceremony and for the rest of the day, so feel free to snap away to your heart's content!

Ladies and gentlemen, would you please be upstanding for the arrival of the bridal party?

(Music for Lindsey's arrival – Let It Go, Dominic Spencer.)

Would you all please be seated.

INTRODUCTION

Good afternoon everyone. Welcome to the beautiful surroundings of Orocco Pier and welcome to Lindsey and Robert's special day! My name is XXXXXX and I am a Celebrant from the Humanist Society of Scotland and I was delighted when I was asked to conduct today's ceremony.

It is a great pleasure to welcome you all here on this happy occasion and I would like to thank you all, on Robert and Lindsey's behalf, for being here to help them celebrate their big day. They are both delighted to have the people they love and laugh with all in the same room to witness their special day.

I know that some of you have made a huge effort to be here today, in particular Robert's parents who have travelled from Florida, his aunt XXXXX from Alabama and friends XXXX and XXXXX who have come all the way from Australia, but whether you are from near or far, your presence here today is very much appreciated.

Some of you may not have been to a Humanist wedding before and Robert and Lindsey chose this style of ceremony in order to celebrate their marriage in a way that is personal and uniquely special, reflecting who they are as people and how they live their lives together.

Humanism is a life-stance based on freedom of choice and thought. It holds that we have one life and the duty to make the most of it, while respecting the beliefs of others, and to have a care for our environment in the name of future generations. Humanism focuses on those things which unite us all rather than those which divide us – and one of the most important things is to celebrate the love between two people who have decided to make a lasting commitment to one another.

I'd now like to introduce the fine people supporting the bride and groom today. Lindsey's gorgeous bridesmaid is her close friend XXXX and the very pretty flower girl is Robert's niece XXXX. Robert's best man is XXXX and I gather these two have been best friends for around 15 years, so given the fact they've known each other for such a long time, I'm sure there will be no end of funny stories for the speeches later on! And we can't forget about the wonderful job that Lindsey's brother XXXX and Robert's brother-in-law XXXX have done as ushers today.

Speaking of special people, in many cultures including our own, it has of course long been a tradition for the bride to be 'given away'. I know that Lindsey's dad XXXX is very proud and happy today and it will have been an honour for him to escort his daughter down the aisle on this occasion.

Marriage is all about supporting and being there for each other through good times and bad, through happiness and sorrow, whether the going be easy or difficult. Of course Robert and Lindsey have already started their journey on that road of togetherness, but before we move on to the next part of the ceremony perhaps this would be an opportune moment to reflect upon the events that brought these two people to this important point in their lives.

ROBERT AND LINDSEY'S STORIES

Robert and Lindsey's adventure began six years ago at Real Radio.

They first met on a dreary Sunday afternoon when Robert had been called in to do some electrical testing at the news desk. He thought at the weekend he would have the place to himself so he could get his head down and work away, as he says anyone who knows a radio journalist knows they are a nightmare to work with.

However, his calm was shattered when the door to the news room was flung open and in walked a journalist. Robert stuck his head up ready to moan at a familiar face but he was confronted by an extremely pretty red head, who looked like she wanted to be there even less than he did. Lindsey grunted a hello and sat down at her desk putting her headphones on and said nothing to Robert the rest of the day.

Robert immediately got up and ran through to the studio to ask the presenter who the 'hot girl' in the news was. He informed Robert that her name was Lindsey and she was freelancing at the weekend, and used to do a lot of TV work.

After that Robert was very curious about the mysterious girl. She was almost as grumpy as him but was very, very good looking!

Over the years, Lindsey and Robert bonded over their wicked (and some may say sick) sense of humour, they would flirt, (so Lindsey says- as Robert claims he doesn't know how to), and would often crack jokes in the news room that only they found funny.

After a few years of being 'Ships in the night' by complete accident Robert managed to text Lindsey with a text meant for another girl.

Robert was a little startled to see when she replied with: 'Who's This?', he then realised he had made a mistake.

Robert didn't make Lindsey any the wiser and the pair continued to chat over text. He then mustered the courage (knowing Lindsey had clearly had a drink that night) to invite her out.

However, their first date wasn't a success and months passed without them seeing each other- until one day Lindsey burst back into the news room.

Lindsey realised what she had been missing and so she emailed Robert straight away inviting him to go to see the movie 'Ted' with her.

Robert was delighted and excited she wanted to see him and so he told her he would happily go and see a foul mouthed teddy bear with her.

Thankfully this date was a complete success, it ended with a wee snog and was the beginning of a magical time together.

THREE THINGS WE LIKE ABOUT EACH OTHER

In preparing for today's ceremony, I asked Robert and Lindsey to tell me three things that they love about each other. **(Robert and Lindsey Read These out)**

Robert:

I love how Lindsey has two different sides to her. On the surface she is very headstrong and mature. Lindsey has a sharp tongue, a wicked wit and a very dark sense of humour. Underneath she has very innocent qualities. She is extremely kind, and has a massive heart. Lindsey loves animals, she believes in Christmas, she loves Disney World. I love all these things I see in her.

I love Lindsey's optimistic attitude. She fills the house with Self-Help books, and very much takes on the same outlook herself. She is very much a dreamer, and she believes that even thinking positively will result in positive results. When I have no confidence or self esteem, I always think of Lindsey's mindset and push myself into situations I would normally shy away from.

I love how Lindsey's hands are in proportion with mine. My whole life I have had tiny hands for a man, and when holding Lindsey's hand for the first time- I knew it was meant to be… Both our hands are in proportion for each other :)

Lindsey:

I love how everyday you show me how much I mean to you. You tell me how much you love me and you do little things that make me smile like putting my jammies over the radiator before bed, or each time you come back from the bathroom in the middle of the night you kiss me good night.

I also love your optimism and how you embrace any opportunity with a childlike enthusiasm- you always try and find the positive in anyone or any situation and everyday you inspire me to be a better person.

You have such a kind heart, intelligent mind and wicked sense of humour and you make me feel like an equal in every way in our relationship and you always support me no matter what drama I have to deal with.

I even love your OCD as I often use it to my advantage- usually when the hoovering needs done or the bathroom needs cleaned. I plant the seed and watch you obsess over it, then you spring into action and go do it. Haha

ROBERT & LINDSEY'S ENGAGEMENT STORY

In terms of their engagement, well, after a vodka-fuelled day by the pool in Tenerife, Robert and Lindsey decided they wanted to tie the knot.

The plane hadn't even reached the tarmac in Glasgow when Lindsey started to design her engagement ring. Six weeks later Lindsey's beautiful ring arrived and now it was up to Robert to come up with a novel way of popping the question.

Lindsey hates surprises however, so Robert told her he had booked dinner at Cameron House that weekend. Lindsey got all excited as she knew that was the night she would finally get engaged by the beautiful banks of Loch Lomond. How WRONG she could be.

You see Lindsey has always said the place where she actually fell in love with Robert was Glasgow Royal Infirmary. Two days after their successful first date, Lindsey was rushed to hospital while on late shift at Real Radio.

Robert ran to the hospital to find a trembling Lindsey in casualty who was facing surgery. He calmed her down and stayed with her all night until doctors kicked him out around 5.30am. Lindsey says it was that night she knew Robert would change her life forever- as he was the one.

So the day of the marriage proposal arrived and as Lindsey finished her work she got a call from Robert. He told her he had broken his arm at his martial arts class and was at Glasgow Royal Infirmary.

Now for those of you who know Lindsey really well this didn't go down too well with her. That's because she thought her romantic Cameron House dinner and getting engaged to Robert was now out of the question that night. In a rage she drove up to the hospital, thinking how could Robert have been so stupid. There she found him at the door of the hospital with a sling on his arm and a bunch of flowers. She couldn't stop at the door as an ambulance was at her back so she shouted at Robert to get in the car.

The rain was chucking it down and now Robert's plan to propose at the hospital was foiled. As they drove away he panicked and told her to stop the car where he told her he loved her and asked for her hand in marriage as he had the ring tucked in his sling. So Lindsey said yes in a bus lane in Alexandra Parade in Glasgow.

They then drove to their flat which was covered in flowers and the champagne was one ice. However, it took Lindsey another 10 minutes to realise Robert's arm break was indeed fake and his sling was made out of a paper table cloth.

Lindsey did get her Cameron House dinner that night, but most importantly, the pair got engaged and here we are today.

I'm sure you were all delighted to hear about their engagement and you're just as delighted to be here to celebrate their marriage this afternoon.

One person who knows Lindsey and Robert very well is their friend XXXXX XXXX.

XXXXX is used to writing songs for Radio breakfast shows but today he has penned one just for the happy couple's big day.

They just hope it's a clean song XXXXXX..

(Song performed by XXXXXX)

Thanks XXXXXX! That was great!

We have now come to the most important part of the ceremony, when the vows of commitment will be exchanged. I know that Robert and Lindsey have thought seriously about their marriage and that in making these promises, their words will be heartfelt and genuine.

Lindsey, would you please pass your flowers to XXXX and join hands please?

(Lindsey to pass flowers to XXXX and join hands)

Robert and Lindsey, today, on your wedding day, as you promise to love each other forever, you are holding the hands of your best friend. These are the hands that will work alongside yours, as together you build your future. These are the hands that will passionately love you and cherish you through the years. These are the hands that will give you strength and support when you need it. And as your hands are joined together now, so may your hearts always be.

Robert and Lindsey stand here today, in the presence of their closest friends and family, to make a lifelong commitment to each other and they are now going to exchange their vows.

(I'll give you a card to read from)

Lindsey:

"Today our amazing adventure continues and I will marry my best friend.
You are the one I live with, laugh with and will love forever.
I may frustrate you and deserve the odd monkey rub on occasion but I will do my best to listen to you, encourage, support, and care for you.
I may even let you win the odd argument ;0)
I promise to give you the very best of me and I will continue to share with you my feelings, fears, secrets and dreams.
You are the first and only person I've ever loved and the first person who ever truly loved me and I can't wait to spend the rest of my life with you.

I've finally found my Disney prince."

Robert:

"Lindsey, over our years together you have been the most difficult struggle I have ever had to work at.
I am constantly pushed to become a better person. I undertake a challenge head on and I can happily say that for the rest of my life, I will truly enjoy endeavouring to be the best partner and husband I can be.

I have my team mate, my best buddy, my voice of reason and my play pal all rolled into one beautiful, beautiful person.

I can't wait to share our life adventures together. This is only the start.

Lindsey you make me happier than I could ever imagine and I am more loved than I have ever thought possible....it is a dream come true. You are my soul mate and I am blessed and privileged to be a part of you life."

Robert and Lindsey, you have bound yourselves together by these commitments and the bond is made by your love for one another.

I'd now like to welcome Robert's sister, XXXXXX, to undertake the hand fasting.

You have bound yourselves together by these vows and in token of that bond, this hand fasting ties the knot.

I now join your hands in physical union. May your union bear you up together.

(XXXXX to put the sash/ribbon under the couple's hands and raises them slightly)

This bond is made by Robert's love for Lindsey

(first wrap)

This bond is made by Lindsey's love for Robert

(second wrap)

This bond is sealed by the love that we all have for you and for our great joy in your union. And as this cloth binds your hands, so too may your hearts be joined.

A hand fasting is no knot of steel. Robert and Lindsey are not handcuffed to each other by force. It is not a sailor's knot that will never slip. But this is a strong knot because it is the will of Robert and Lindsey to make it so.

May it never come undone under the strain of the storms of life.

May it sit lightly and pleasantly upon you that you may walk through life hand in hand, mind with mind, and heart to heart.

And now for your legal declarations of marriage.

Lindsey, would you please repeat the following words after me:

"I Lindsey Jean Archibald solemnly and sincerely accept you, Robert Graham Crumlish in marriage."

And Robert, would you please repeat the following words after me:

"I Robert Graham Crumlish solemnly and sincerely accept you, Lindsey Jean Archibald in marriage."

Lindsey and Robert will now exchange rings as a symbol of their commitment and the rings have been very carefully looked after by XXXX so can I have them brought forward please?

Robert and Lindsey, your wedding rings will stand as a permanent reminder of the vows you have exchanged today. Wear them always and when you look at them, think about each other and remember the happiness you felt on this, your wedding day.

Lindsey, would you place the ring on Robert's left hand, and repeat after me:

"Robert, I join my life with yours today without hesitation and with an open and trusting heart. Take this ring and with it my commitment to be the best wife I can be."

And Robert, could you place the ring on Lindsey's left hand and repeat after me:

"Lindsey, I place this ring on your finger as a token of my enduring love and from this day forward we shall be as one."

Robert and Lindsey, now that you have exchanged your vows of commitment and your wedding rings, in the presence of your family, friends and witnesses, I have much pleasure in declaring you married and pronouncing you husband and wife! You may share your first kiss!!

(Pause for kissing, clapping and cheering!)

It was important to Robert and Lindsey that their parents play an important role today, as their parents are very important people in their lives. They have always been there for them, have always looked after them and put their needs first, and have shaped them into the honest, caring and hard working people that you see before you today.

With this in mind, Robert and Lindsey wish to say an extra special thank you to their mums, to thank them for the many sacrifices they have made, for being the constant strength in their life and for their unconditional love and support, and I'd now like to ask you both a question on their behalf.

XXXX and XXXXX, would you do Lindsey and Robert the honour of being the witnesses for the signing of their marriage schedule this afternoon?

"We do"

During this time, we will be listening to some music and I hope that this will give each of you the opportunity to reflect on the commitment that Lindsey and Robert have made today. If you bear with us, we'll be back to continue with the rest of the ceremony in a few minutes.

Music – Selection from MP3 Player
(Signing of Marriage Schedule)
(Robert and Lindsey to stand together to the left of xxxxx after signing)

Thank you for your attention everyone! I know that you'll all want to join me in offering our heartfelt congratulations and good wishes to Robert and Lindsey. To wish the happy couple all the best in their married lives, I'd now like to invite Robert's dad XXXX to come and read 'Only once in Your Life' for us please.

ROBERT'S DAD:

Only once in your life, I truly believe, you find someone who can completely turn your world around. You tell them things that you've never shared with another soul and they absorb everything you say and actually want to hear more.

When something wonderful happens, you can't wait to tell them about it, knowing they will share in your excitement. They are not embarrassed to cry with you when you are hurting or laugh with you when you make a fool of yourself.

Never do they hurt your feelings or make you feel like you are not good enough, but rather they build you up and show you the things about yourself that make you special and even beautiful.

There is never any pressure, jealousy or competition but only a quiet calmness when they are around. You can be yourself and not worry about what they will think of you because they love you for who you are.

The things that seem insignificant to most people such as a note, song or walk become invaluable treasures kept safe in your heart to cherish forever. Memories of your childhood come back and are so clear and vivid it's like being young again. Colours seem brighter and more brilliant. Laughter seems part of daily life where before it was infrequent or didn't exist at all.

A phone call or two during the day helps to get you through a long day's work and always brings a smile to your face. In their presence, there's no need for continuous conversation, but you find you're quite content in just having them nearby.

Things that never interested you before become fascinating because you know they are important to this person who is so special to you. You think of this person on every occasion and in everything you do. Simple things bring them to mind like a pale blue sky, gentle wind or even a storm cloud on the horizon.

You open your heart knowing that there's a chance it may be broken one day and in opening your heart, you experience a love and joy that you never dreamed possible. You find that being vulnerable is the only way to allow your heart to feel true pleasure that's so real it scares you.

You find strength in knowing you have a true friend and possibly a soul mate who will remain loyal to the end. Life seems completely different, exciting and worthwhile. Your only hope and security is in knowing that they are a part of your life.

Thanks xxxx. Lovely words there!

Robert and Lindsey would love to have a group photograph take of all of their guests after the ceremony so please listen out for instructions from the photographer.

To bring the ceremony to a close, I'd like to end with a verse of well wishing to reflect all of our good wishes today.

Robert and Lindsey:

May your home be a place of happiness for all who enter it;
a place where the old and young are renewed in each other's company,
a place for growing and a place for sharing,
a place for music, a place for laughter and a place for love.

Robert and Lindsey, now that you are married, go forward in your life together, with the warm good wishes of all of us here today. We wish you much happiness. May life smile upon you and may all of your days together be as the stars in the sky - numerous and bright.

On behalf of Lindsey and Robert, I would like to thank all of you for coming here today and I hope you enjoy the rest of the celebrations.

Can I now please ask you to be upstanding for the bride and groom?

Ladies and gentlemen, it now gives me great pleasure to present to you, the happily married couple, Robert and Lindsey who are now officially Mr and Mrs Crumlish!

(Music for exit – Time After Time, by Dominic Spencer.)

(You exit to applause and big, beaming smiles – and live happily ever after!)

Chapter 36: Top 15 websites and apps for wedding planning

WE now live in a digital age and thankfully there are lots of great websites and apps that can help with your wedding planning.

Here are a few of my favourites that helped reduce my stress levels:

Wedding Planning App

When we were keeping tabs on all the things we had booked and how much we had already paid we just used an Excel spreadsheet to keep things simple. However, there are lots of cool apps you can download on your phone to keep you right. Just type in 'wedding planning' into your App store and choose one, I liked one called 'iWedPlanner' as it was really good to use as it had everything you needed to think about for your big day.

Weddingquotes2u.co.uk

As I've mentioned a few times in this book, planning a wedding can cost a fortune. To help save some pennies we used www.weddingquotes2u.co.uk to get some prices from various vendors. The site allows you to compare prices with wedding professionals up and down the country- they offer everything from car hire, photography, flowers, music to hair and beauty. It's a one stop shop.

photographers4me.co.uk

This website is how we found our amazing photographer for our wedding for just £350. You log on and pop in when your big day will take place and where it will be held then you put in a total cost of what you are willing to pay. However, it's then up to photographers to bid for your business and you will receive emails with quotes as they all try to outbid each other.

Facebook

We used Facebook from the moment we started planning our big day. It was just brilliant for keeping in touch with most of our guests. We set up a page for the wedding countdown then we set up a further two pages to help organise the stag and hen nights. We then updated them regularly with our journey to becoming man and wife as well as informing our guests with all the vital arrangements.

Wedding Websites

To keep your guests all up to date with your journey many couples set up their own wedding websites. There are lots of sites online which you can just join and choose a template which will allow you to post what you want. Most will offer a basic free service (which is all you need) but many will offer you an upgraded package for a one off fee. Popular websites include www.gettingmarried.co.uk and www.appycouple.com where you not only customise your own website, but you also create your very own app. Prices start from $35.

Amazon

We use Amazon all the time and it really came in handy for some of our wedding planning. We hopped on and bought all our candy buffet equipment as well as things like table diamonds and other accessories.

Amazon is also great if you want to set up a wedding gift wish list. You can create a list of all the things you would like to receive from your guests and then you can post the link onto your wedding Facebook page for them to have a look at.

Hobbycraft

We used hobbycraft.co.uk to buy little things for the wedding such as our party poppers and bubbles. However, the store has quite an extensive range of wedding accessories to help you plan your big day. If you don't want to just order online you can also visit one of their many stores dotted across the country.

Evernote

During the last month in the run up to the wedding we used the Evernote app on our phones virtually every day. My husband and I shared documents and our to-do list and each time one of us completed a wedding task then we ticked it off the list. I think this app is really handy when you are constantly on the go and you want to keep track of things.

Skype

My husband's family live in America so communicating with them via Skype is essential and when we were in the midst of planning our big day it was great to keep them included via video link.

It's also a great tool for on your wedding day if you have guests who can't make it. You can hook up to them via Skype and let them join in part of the festivities, especially if they live on the other side of the world.

Pinterest

This is a great website for gathering ideas for your wedding. You can collect anything from wedding dress designs, colour schemes, stationery templates and hair and beauty ideas. It's a great way to collect all your creative ideas all in the once place for you and your other half to consider for your big day.

Myfitnesspal

Both my husband and I wanted to lose a bit of weight for our wedding as we wanted to look and feel great on our big day. The myfitnesspal app came in really handy as we could keep track of our calories as well as how much we were exercising by using the app. You can also put all your measurements and weight into the app and when you tell it how much weight you want to lose it will then tell you how many calories a day you should be eating.

Wedding Accessories

I found a great website for glitzy wedding accessories called www.crystalbridalaccessories.co.uk It's where I got my necklace and earring set which cost me £75- the jewellery was just beautiful. The online store has designs to suit all tastes and budgets. They also do other accessories such as tiaras, shoes and bridal handbags. Well worth the visit.

Stationery

We initially got our wedding invitations made by a woman we met at a wedding fayre. However, at a very late stage we discovered we hadn't invited certain people so we decided just to order more invitations online from a store called www.brideandgroomdirect.co.uk They have a huge selection of beautiful wedding stationery in all different shapes, sizes and colours that will meet any budget. We also bought our thank you cards from that website as well as our wedding guest book we passed around our reception.

Booking.com

When it came to organising accommodation for all our guests this website was invaluable. All you do is type in the location of where you want to stay and the date you want to go and it will search all the available hotels and bed and breakfasts for you. We popped the link on our wedding Facebook page and we let our guests book where they wanted to stay.

Wedding countdown app

There are lots of wedding countdown apps that you can download for your phone. They are a great accessory. All you do is type in the date of when you are getting married and then it automatically starts counting down to your big day. When I reached various milestones I used to take a screen grab and post it on to my social media accounts. Now that I am married my counter is counting down to our first wedding anniversary.

Chapter 37: Live happily ever after!

OUR wedding day really was the best day of our lives. We had all the people we love and laugh with all in the same room and, unfortunately, there are very few happy occasions in your life when that can happen.

During our wedding planning journey we made some mistakes, paid more than we should have and had some blazing rows in the process. However, in our eyes, our wedding was just the most perfect occasion and one we will never forget. And now we are both on an incredible new journey.

When it is your turn to get married I think it is important to realise that you can never afford to stop paying attention to your relationship. Marriage is hard work, and you have to work at it every day.

When the two of you first got together, you spent time and emotional energy to become close. You shared your thoughts, feelings and experiences with one another. Over time, people become guilty of not nurturing their relationships because they have so many other pressing responsibilities. There's a job, housework, and children to tend to.

But you owe it to yourself and your spouse to give your relationship special care. Relationships are like anything else in life- if you put the hard work in then you will get the awesome rewards.

And hopefully this wedding planning guide will get you off to the best possible start.

Good luck with married life, it's awesome!

The Bunny Club

If you would like to be part of the Bunny Boiler to Bride relationship club then head to my website **www.bunnyboilertobride.com**

Each week in the Bunny Club you will be given FREE advice on how to maintain a great relationship as well as tips on how to boost your sex life, advice on how to keep your crazy in the box, and how you can learn to become the woman all men want, not the one they feel they have to put up with.

Join the Bunny Club today by heading to my website:

www.bunnyboilertobride.com

or

Follow Lindsey on Twitter @LindsArchibald

www.ingramcontent.com/pod-product-compliance
Lightning Source LLC
Chambersburg PA
CBHW071220280526
45787CB00002B/745